i Think: E   s

Personal Finance

By Kendra Corr

With contributions by Wendy Moeller

© InspirEd Educators, Inc.   Atlanta, Georgia

** It is the goal of InspirEd Educators to create instructional materials that are interesting, engaging, and challenging. Our student-centered approach incorporates both content and skills, placing particular emphasis on reading, writing, vocabulary development, and critical and creative thinking in the content areas.

Edited by Kendra Corr and Sharon Coletti

Cover graphics by Sharon Coletti and Print1 Direct

Copyright © 2009 by InspirEd Educators, Inc.

ISBN # 978-1-933558-80-6

Printed in the United States of America

About InspirEd Educators

InspirEd Educators was founded in 2000 by author Sharon Coletti. Our mission is to provide interesting, student-centered, and thought-provoking instructional materials. To accomplish this, we design lesson plans with research-based content information presented in various ways and used as the vehicle for developing critical and creative thinking, reading, writing, collaboration, problem-solving, and other necessary and enduring skills. By requiring students to THINK, our lessons ensure FAR greater retention than simple memorization of facts!

Initially our company offered large, comprehensive, multi-disciplinary social studies curricula. Then in 2008 we joined forces with another small company and author, Kendra Corr, and launched a second line of thematic units, many excerpted and adapted from our original products. These flexible and affordable resources are ideal for individual, small, or large-group instruction. We hope you will find our company's unique approach valuable and that we can serve you again in the near future.

If you are interested in our other offerings, you can find information on our main website at **www.inspirededucators.com**. Additional products are also available at **www.inspiredhomeschoolers.com**.

InspirEd Educators materials provide engaging lesson plans that vary daily and include:

- Lesson-specific Springboards (warm-ups)
- Writing Activities
- Critical and creative thinking
- Problem-solving
- Test-taking skill development
- Primary source analyses (DBQ's)
- Multiple perspectives
- Graphic analyses
- Fascinating readings
- Simulations
- Story-telling
- Practical use of technology
- Debates
- Plays
- Research
- Graphic organizers
- AND SO MUCH MORE!!!!!

Thank you for choosing our units,
Sharon Coletti, President
InspirEd Educators

Tips for Teaching with InspirEd Educators Units

- Before beginning the unit, take time to look through the Objectives and lessons. This will give you a chance to think about what you want to emphasize and decide upon any modifications, connections, or extensions you'd like to include.

- Give your student(s) the Objective worksheet at the beginning of unit study. The Objectives serve as an outline of the content to be covered and provide a means to review information. Have your student(s) define the terms as they progress through the lessons and thoroughly answer the essential questions. You can check responses as you go along or wait and check everything as a test review. It is important that your student(s) have some opportunity to receive feedback on their Objective answers, since assessments provided at the end of the unit are based on these.

- Read through each lesson's materials before beginning. This will help you better understand lesson concepts; decide when and how to present the vocabulary and prepare the handouts (or transparencies) you will need.

- "Terms to know" can be introduced at the beginning of lessons or reviewed at the end, unless specified otherwise. (In a few instances the intent is for students to discover the meanings of the terms.)

- Look over what we have given you and use whatever you feel your student(s) need. Suggestions are sometimes offered for enrichment, but feel free to use any lesson as a jumping-off point to pursue other topics of interest.

- Our materials are intended to prompt discussion. Often students' answers may vary, but it's important that they be able to substantiate their opinions and ideas with facts. Let the discussion flow!

- Note that differentiated assessments are provided at the end of the unit. Feel free to use any of these as appropriate; cut-and-paste to revise, or create your own tests as desired.

- For additional information and research sites refer to the Resource Section in the back of the unit.

- InspirEd Educators units are all about thinking and creativity, so allow yourself the freedom to adapt the materials as you see fit. Our goal is to provide a springboard for you to jump from in your teaching and your student(s)' learning.

- ENJOY! We at InspirEd Educators truly believe that teaching and learning should be enjoyable, so we do our best to make our lessons interesting and varied. We want you and your student(s) to love learning!

Table of Contents

Personal Finance Objectives

Vocabulary – Be able to define and use the following terms:

- personal finance
- goal
- asset
- liability
- pay scale
- salary
- career
- poverty rate
- budget
- income
- mortgage
- insurance
- living expenses
- tuition
- utilities
- retailer
- internship
- benefits
- commission
- checking account
- deposit
- withdrawal
- consumer
- deceptive
- endorse
- credit
- interest
- statement
- credit rating
- credit score
- credit report
- bankruptcy
- loan officer
- down payment
- closing costs
- identity theft
- scam
- retirement
- investment
- return
- maturation
- economy
- recession
- foreclosure
- reflection

Fully answer the following questions:

1. Explain why personal goal setting and education are important to finances.
2. Explain the usefulness and value of budgets.
3. Describe the various ways someone can get paid.
4. Explain the purpose of checking accounts and how to use one wisely.
5. Describe deceptive advertising and explain how it can hurt consumers.
6. Explain what someone should know about using credit cards.
7. Describe how a credit rating can help or keep someone from getting a loan.
8. Explain how identity theft happens and how to avoid it.
9. Describe the various ways money can be saved and invested.
10. Describe how the state of the economy can affect individuals.

Vocabulary - Be able to define and use the following terms:

Definitions for terms are provided in the lessons in which they are introduced.

Fully answer the following questions:

1. Setting long and short term goals helps plan for the future. Personal finance impacts whether or not people meet their personal goals. There is a direct link between educational attainment and earnings potential, so education should definitely be part of any plan to achieve success.

2. A budget is a practical way to see what is spent versus what is earned. People generally have three types of expenses that should be budgeted: fixed, variable, and discretionary items.

3. People's earnings, or incomes, are not only the dollars they receive in a paycheck. Benefits such as insurance and perks such as day care also have value that should be considered.

4. Checking accounts make it easy to deposit and withdraw money and are often used to pay bills and day-to-day expenses with debit cards. Checking activity must be monitored and recorded to avoid expensive overdraft fees. If there is consistently extra money at the end of the month or pay period, it might be wise to open a savings account as well.

5. Deceptive advertising techniques include: bait and switch or luring consumers into buying something more expensive than what was advertised; misleading endorsements by celebrities; and false pricing and sales. These practices get consumers to buy products under false pretenses.

6. Credit cards can be dangerous if they lead to overspending or unnecessary splurges. The fees and interest can add up quickly, making the original purchases cost more. Credit cards should be used with caution, for emergencies, or for purchases that can be paid off before interest charges occur. In general they should not be used for what a person cannot afford!

7. Credit ratings (made up among other things, of a credit report and score) are used by lenders to get a picture of people's financial habits to make decisions about making loans. In addition to getting loans, a good credit rating can result in better interest rates, which can save a lot of money over the life of a loan.

8. Identity theft is when thieves steal personal information (such as a social security number, banking information, or credit card numbers) to make illegal purchases, steal money, or set up credit in the victim's name without his/her knowledge or permission. Safeguarding paperwork, mail, trash, and computer files can greatly lessen the chances of becoming a victim of this type of crime.

9. Money can be saved in savings accounts or cafeteria plans or invested in the stock market, retirement accounts, mutual funds, 401K's, and the like. In all cases the investor should consider the potential risk of losing money and the rate of return, or profit, made from the investment.

10. The economy generally follows a business cycle in which conditions and activity either speed up as in recovery or peak times or slow down in recessions. Individuals can be affected by these trends in terms of job gain or loss, ease of obtaining credit, ability to spend and invest, and general feelings of confidence or fear.

S-U-C-C-E-S-S!

Springboard:
Students should complete the "What is Success?"
free write for 3-5 minutes..
(Answers will vary but should spark discussion.)

Objective: The student will be able to explain why it is important to set personal goals.

Materials: What is Success? (Springboard handout)
Setting Your Goals (handout)
Brainstorm! (handout)
Assets and Liabilities (handout - see below)

Terms to know: **personal finance** - money decisions made by and affecting an individual person
goal - what is hoped to be achieved in the future
asset - factor that helps goals to be met
liability - factor that stands in the way in meeting your goals

Procedure:

- After sharing their Springboard answers, explain that _in this unit the student(s) will learn how personal finance (review term) can help achieve success_. Go on to explain that _in order to achieve success one should make a plan for "getting there," whatever "there" means in terms of success for each person. One way to do this is to set goals for the future._

- Distribute "Setting Your Goals" and review the directions. The student(s) should work independently to identify short-term and long-term goals.

- Have them share their goals, as desired.

- Then distribute "Brainstorm!" and have the student(s) work individually, in pairs, or small groups to brainstorm per handout directions.

- Have them share / compare their ideas and discuss. *(Answers will vary but should be explained.)*

- Introduce the terms "asset" and "liability" and explain that _though these terms can be used in a strictly financial way, referring to wealth and property or debts, this unit uses more general definitions. Assets can be ANYTHING that can help achieve goals (talent, skills, saving money, etc.), and liabilities can be ANYTHING that stands in their way (debt, poor credit, uncooperative attitude, etc)._

- Distribute "Assets and Liabilities." Explain that _the student(s) will begin filling in this organizer now and continue to record ideas throughout the unit of study_. Have them add one example from this lesson and discuss. *(Answers will vary, but setting clear goals can be an asset because they provide a "blueprint" or plan for working toward and achieving success.)*

What Is Success?

DIRECTIONS: Freewrite to answer the questions below. When you freewrite, you just start writing and keep writing until you're told to stop! This is a kind of brainstorming session, so spelling, grammar and punctuation are not relevant at this point. Just let your ideas FLOW!

What does "success" mean to you?

How will you know when you have achieved success?

_____

_____

_____

_____

_____

_____

_____

_____

_____

_____

_____

_____

_____

_____

_____

_____

_____

_____

_____

_____

_____

_____

Setting Your Goals

DIRECTIONS: Read the information below. Then list and explain AT LEAST TWO long term goals and AT LEAST FIVE short term goals that you have for your future.

> To achieve all you want, it is helpful to set goals. There are two types of goals. **Long term goals** are those you must work toward over a long period of time. These won't happen overnight, but take time and careful planning to achieve. **Short term goals** can be accomplished in less time and can often be "steps" that can lead to a long term goal.

Long Term Goals:

1. _____

_____

_____

2. _____

_____

_____

_____

Another? _____

_____

_____

Short Term Goals:

1. _____

_____

_____

2. _____

_____

_____

3. _____

_____

_____

4. _____

_____

_____

5. _____

_____

_____

Another? _____

_____

_____

Many things you do can help you meet your goals, while others stand in your way. Brainstorm a list for each category. Be prepared to explain your ideas!

How to HELP meet your goals	OBSTACLES to meeting your goals
_____	_____
_____	_____
_____	_____
_____	_____
_____	_____
_____	_____
_____	_____
_____	_____
_____	_____
_____	_____
_____	_____
_____	_____
_____	_____
_____	_____
_____	_____
_____	_____
_____	_____
_____	_____

↑ ASSETS AND LiABiLiTiES ↓

DIRECTIONS: As you progress through the unit, add and explain examples of assets and liabilities -- what you learn that can HELP meet your goals and what might HURT your chances of meeting them.

Powerful Stuff!

Springboard:
Students should complete the "Help Wanted" handout.
(Answers will vary but should be justified and spark discussion.)

Objective: The student will be able to explain the link between education and earning power.

Materials:
    Help Wanted (Springboard handout)
    Sources Tell Us... (2-page handout)
    Dissecting the Data (handout)
    Do Your Research (handout)

Terms to know:
    pay scale - list of salaries based on experience, education, years on the job, or other factors
    salary - fixed amount of money earned in a year, paid at regular intervals
    career - long-term job or occupation
    poverty rate - percentage of people who are poor

Procedure:

- After reviewing the Springboard, explain that *this lesson examines the link between education and money earned*.

- Distribute the "Sources Tell Us..." and 'Dissecting the Data" handouts. The student(s) should work individually, in pairs, or small groups to study the data and complete the analysis form. (**NOTE:** For many students it may be necessary to review the difference between the degrees listed in the data, particularly the number of years it takes to earn each.)

- Have the student(s) share and compare their ideas and discuss.

- Distribute "Do Your Research." Explain that *the student(s) should pick a possible career that is of interest to them. These might be among the things listed in the previous goal-setting lesson or unrelated*.

- Using the research guide provided, the student(s) should use the Internet to learn the requirements for pursuing that career and how much money could be expected. (**FYI:** There are several websites devoted to this topic. A search for "career information for students" nets good results. One particularly good site is the Occupational Outlook Handbook located at the U.S. Bureau of Labor Statistics homepage @ **www.bls.gov/oco**.)

- Have the student(s) share what they learn and add ideas to their "Assets and Liabilities" organizer. *(Possible assets could be job training or education; liabilities could be dropping out of high school or not finishing college.)*

HELP WANTED

DIRECTIONS: Study the pay scale for teachers in Riverview School District and the profiles of three people applying for the job. Then decide who you would hire and explain your decision in the space provided.

Years Experience	Bachelor's Degree	Master's Degree	Doctorate Degree
0-3	$35,000	$37,000	$40,000
4-9	$38,000	$42,000	$45,000
10-15	$42,000	$46,000	$50,000
15+	$46,000	$50,000	$55,000

The first candidate for the position is **Mr. Jackson**, a brand new teacher right out of college with a Bachelor's degree in education with a C+ average in his college courses. He is also qualified to coach varsity football and would love to do so.

The second applicant is **Ms. Springfield**, who has moved in from out-of-state and is seeking a teaching job near her new home. She has sixteen years of experience and comes with excellent recommendations from her former district. She has a doctorate degree in education and maintained an A average throughout her university career.

The third option is **Mr. Tucker**. He earned a Master's degree in education and also has a Bachelor's degree in psychology, maintaining a B average in all his studies. He has been teaching for nine years and is interested in sponsoring an afterschool program to help at-risk students.

I would hire _____ because:

_____

_____

_____

_____

_____

_____

Why do you think teachers with higher degrees earn more money in this district? _____

_____

_____

_____

_____

Sources Tell Us...

Source #1 - National Center for Education Statistics, Outcomes of Education Report, 2000

Average Salary According to Level of Educational Achievement

Education Level	Men	Women
Less than 9th grade	$20,789	$15,978
Some High School	$25,095	$17,919
High school diploma or G.E.D.	$34,303	$24,970
Some college	$40,337	$28,697
2 year Associates Degree	$41,952	$31,071
Bachelor's Degree	$56,334	$40,415
Master's Degree	$68,332	$50,139
Professional Degree (pharmacist, lawyer, veterinarian)	$99,411	$58,957
Doctorate Degree	$80,250	$57,081

Source #2 - MSN Money, 2006

Average Additional Dollars Earned over 40 Years Compared to a Person with a High School Diploma

Degree	Average Value Added
Associate's	$116,550
Bachelor's	$308,588
Master's	$180,010
Doctorate	$187,920
Professional	$716,927

Source #3 - Bureau of Labor Statistics, 2009

The Top Ten Highest Paid Jobs in 2009 (base salary shown)

#1	Anesthesiologist	$184,340
#2	Surgeon	$184,150
#3	Obstetrician and Gynecologist	$178,040
#4	Orthodontist	$176,900
#5	Oral Surgeon	$164,760
#6	Internist (specialist doctor)	$160,860
#7	Prosthodontist (dental specialist)	$158,940
#8	Psychiatrist	$149,990
#9	General Practitioner (family doctor)	$149,850
#10	Chief Executive Officer	$144,600

Source #4 - U.S. Census Bureau, 2006 American Community Survey

People Living Below the Poverty Line by Level of Education
(Poverty line is below $20,000 for a family of four)

Education Level	Total % of population	% of male population	% of female population
Less than High School diploma	23.7%	19.5%	27.8%
High school diploma	11.5%	9.3%	13.5%
Some college or Associates Degree	7.8%	6.0%	9.2%
Bachelor's Degree	4.1%	3.6%	4.4%
Bachelor's +	3.1%	2.7%	3.5%

Source #5 - U.S. Census Bureau: American Community Survey, 2006

Unemployment Rate by Level of Education - Age 25-64

Education Level	Unemployment Rate
Less than High School diploma	9.6%
High School diploma	6.1%
Some College or Associates Degree	4.7%
Bachelor's Degree or higher	2.7%

Source #6 - U.S. Census Bureau: Occupational Outlook Quarterly, 2005

Lifetime Earnings Estimates by Level of Education

Education Level	Lifetime Earnings (in 2006 dollars)
Some High School, no degree	$1,000,000
High School diploma	$1,200,000
Some college, no degree	$1,500,000
Associate's Degree	$1,600,000
Bachelor's Degree	$2,100,000
Master's Degree	$2,500,000
Doctoral Degree	$3,400,000
Professional Degree	$4,400,000

Source #7 - Investopedia, a Forbes Digital Company

Three Top Paying Double Majors

#1	Master of Business Administration + Communications
#2	Master of Business Administration + Hospitality
#3	Master of Business Administration + Cultural Anthropology

Dissecting the Data

DIRECTIONS: Decide if each statement is true or false. Then explain why and write the number of the source(s) upon which your answer is based below.

1. _____ The more education you have, the more money you earn.

2. _____ Educated people are more likely to lose their jobs.

3. _____ High school drop outs are more likely to be poor than others.

4. _____ Most highly paid people are in the business field.

5. _____ Higher educated people can retire earlier.

6. _____ The money it costs to go to college is not worth it in the long run.

7. _____ People with more education usually have more money by the time they are 50.

8. _____ It is just as important for women to be educated as men.

9. _____ Quality of life has nothing to do with education.

10. _____ Doctors' incomes have fallen in recent years.

11. _____ Americans earn equal pay for equal work.

12. _____ It is a waste of money to go to college these days.

13._____ The work teachers do is more valuable than the work of business people.

14. _____ It is important to have multiple skills in today's job market.

15. _____ Education can make or break you in America.

Dissecting the Data - Suggestions for Answers

NOTE: *ANSWERS MAY VARY, as long as they are justified and well-reasoned.*

1. _True_ The more education you have, the more money you earn. *Sources 1, 2, and 6 illustrate this point.*

2. _False_ Educated people are more likely to lose their jobs. *Source 5 shows higher unemployment for people with less education, and Source 4 shows higher rates of poverty for people with less education.*

3. _True_ High school drop outs are more likely to be poor than others. *Source 4 shows poverty stats. Also, Source 1 shows that salaries for people with less than a 9th grade education and female high school drop-outs were below the poverty line in 2006.*

4. _False_ Most highly paid people are in the business field. *Source 3 indicates nine out of ten of the highest paid professions are actually in medicine or dentistry.*

5. _True_ Higher educated people can retire earlier. *Source 6 shows that lifetime earnings are higher for highly educated people and Source 2 supports the fact that higher education results in more earnings over 40 years.*

6. _T or F_ The money it costs to go to college is not worth it in the long run. *Sources 2 and 6 show higher degrees bring much higher earnings. But if students think the costs of college are more than added earnings in Source 2, they may disagree.*

7. _True_ People with more education usually have more money by the time they are 50. *Source 1 and 6 both indicate this is so.*

8. _True_ It is just as important for women to be educated as men. *However, it could also be FALSE if seen as __MORE__ critical for women. Source 1 shows women earn less with the same education, and Source 4 shows a higher percentage of poor women.*

9. _False_ Quality of life has nothing to do with education. *Sources 1,2, and 6 all show higher education brings more money, which should bring a higher quality of life. Also, Source 4 shows higher percentages of poverty and Source 5 higher unemployment for uneducated people – logically a lower quality of life.*

10. _False_ Doctor's incomes have fallen in recent years. *Though this may be true, Source 3 indicates 9 out of the 10 of the highest salaries were in a medical field.*

11. _T or F_ Americans earn equal pay for equal work. *Some students may think Source 1 shows lower wages for women regardless of degree, meaning women are not paid as much for men for the same jobs. Others may consider other factors or that level of education isn't an indication of what "work" is being done.*

12. _False_ It is a waste of money to go to college these days. *Source 6 indicates that the cost of college is recovered in higher salaries, which is also supported by Sources 1, 2, and 3.*

13. _False_ The work teachers do is more valuable than the work of business people. *Source 3 shows that other professions are paid more, but many students may argue that the "value" of a career doesn't necessarily translate to high salary.*

14. _True_ It is important to have multiple skills in today's job market. *Source 7 supports this. For example an MBA with a communications degree earns a higher salary than an MBA alone.*

15. _True_ Education can make or break you in America. *Answers will vary. According to the sources, this may seem true, however only ON THE AVERAGE. Some people with little education grow wealthy, while highly educated people earn little.*

DO YOUR RESEARCH!

CAREER INFORMATION

Career Interest:

What do these people do on the job?

What are the working conditions for this career? (office, travel, labor...)

What training and/or education is needed?

What skills are needed?

Typical earnings:

What is the level of demand for this occupation? Are there many positions available?

Anything else?

Stretching a Dollar

Objective: The student will be able to explain the importance of making a budget.

Materials: Spending Survey (1/2 page Springboard handout)
Monthly Budget (handout)
The Bottom Line (handout)

Terms to know: **budget** - a plan for how money will be spent
income - money earned
mortgage - money borrowed to buy a house
insurance - regular payments for protection of a person or family against theft, harm, illness, fire, accidents, or death

Procedure:

· After completing the Springboard survey, have the student(s) tally their scores and determine which profile they fall into:

10 - 20 points: You are a "Pat Pinchpenny." You are very careful with your money and do not take spending lightly! You do research and consider your purchases very seriously before buying. You likely have a healthy savings account, or will one day.

21 - 39 points: You are a "Morgan Middlemoney." You are somewhat careful about big purchases, but quick to spend smaller amounts of money. You probably don't owe much, but are just as likely to not have much saved either.

40 - 50 points: You are a "Sandy Spender." You don't think much about spending your money and even feel you're "missing out" if you don't. You have no savings and likely owe at least one person money at any given time. You have probably made some buying decisions you regret because you either didn't need the item, paid too much for it, or bought something that turned out to be a disappointment.

· Have the student(s) share and discuss their profiles and explain that *in this lesson they will learn about figuring out and living on a budget* (review term).

· Distribute the "Monthly Budget" and "The Bottom Line" handouts. Have the student(s) study the sample budget and complete the analysis as directed.

· Have them share / compare their ideas and discuss. *(Answers will vary; see Teacher page for suggestions.)*

· The student(s) should then add lesson examples to the "Assets and Liabilities" handout. *(Assets include making and sticking to a budget; liabilities would be not making a budget, overspending, etc.)*

20

$pending $urvey

DIRECTIONS: Answer the questions using the following point values:

5 - always true   4 - usually true   3 - sometimes true

2 - rarely true   1 - never true

1. _____ When I get money for a gift, I run out and spend it right away.
2. _____ When I want to buy something, I just buy it without comparing prices.
3. _____ I do not have a savings account that I regularly put money into.
4. _____ I never plan for big purchases; I just borrow the money if I can.
5. _____ I spend a lot of money on candy, soda, and fast food.
6. _____ I couldn't tell you exactly how much money I have.
7. _____ I often have to borrow money from friends or family.
8. _____ I never look at what's on sale before I make purchases.
9. _____ I don't keep my money organized in a wallet; it's everywhere!
10. _____ I am not as careful as I should be about buying quality items.

Your Score: _____

$pending $urvey

DIRECTIONS: Answer the questions using the following point values:

5 - always true   4 - usually true   3 - sometimes true

2 - rarely true   1 - never true

1. _____ When I get money for a gift, I run out and spend it right away.
2. _____ When I want to buy something, I just buy it without comparing prices.
3. _____ I do not have a savings account that I regularly put money into.
4. _____ I never plan for big purchases; I just borrow the money if I can.
5. _____ I spend a lot of money on candy, soda, and fast food.
6. _____ I couldn't tell you exactly how much money I have.
7. _____ I often have to borrow money from friends or family.
8. _____ I never look at what's on sale before I make purchases.
9. _____ I don't keep my money organized in a wallet; it's everywhere!
10. _____ I am not as careful as I should be about buying quality items.

Your Score: _____

Monthly Budget

Monthly Income: $4500.00
Family description: 2 adults, 2 children (ages 6 and 10)

Description	Budgeted Amount	Description	Budgeted Amount
Mortgage payment	$1200.00	Home phone service (landline)	$40.00
Car payment	$350.00	Entertainment (dining out, etc.)	$150.00
Child care - before and after school	$250.00	School lunches	$40.00
Car insurance	$110.00	Pet expenses (food, vet, etc.)	$35.00
Student loan payment	$95.00	Life insurance	$30.00
Cell phones (3)	$150.00	Groceries	$500.00
Internet service	$40.00	Hair/nail care	$85.00
Health club membership	$30.00	Magazine subscriptions	$15.00
Satellite television	$90.00	Babysitter (weekends)	$75.00
Credit card payment	$200.00	Newspaper subscription	$20.00
Gas company	$65.00	Lawn service	$45.00
Electric company	$60.00	Clothing/shoes	$300.00
Trash pickup	$25.00	Water / sewer service	$45.00
Misc. household items	$100.00	House cleaning service	$120.00
Doctor / Dentist visits	$50.00	Medication	$65.00
Health insurance	$150.00	Netflix	$10.00
Piano lessons (for the 10-year-old)	$80.00	Pee Wee football (for the 6-year-old)	$120.00
Gasoline	$400.00	Savings deposit	?????

Total Expenses: $5140.00

The Bottom Line

Which spending profile from the Springboard do you think best fits this family? Why? _____
_____
_____

Explain what this family spends in comparison to what they earn. How can they do this, and what problems could arise as a result? _____
_____
_____
_____

What items do you think the family might spend LESS on than what they have budgeted? What budget items, if any, do you think may be too LOW? _____
_____
_____
_____

List and explain three NEEDS the family must pay for every month ._____
_____
_____
_____
_____

List and explain three budget items the family WANTS, but doesn't have to have.
_____
_____
_____
_____

Why do you think it's important to distinguish between NEEDS and WANTS in budgeting? Explain. _____
_____

What advice would you give this family regarding their financial situation? _____
_____
_____

Do you think making and abiding by a budget is a smart financial habit? Why or why not? _____
_____
_____
_____

Which spending profile from the Springboard do you think best fits this family? Why? *Answers may vary, but most students will likely classify them as "Sandy Spenders." They spend considerably more money than w they earn each month on a wide array of items and do not seem to save anything.*

Explain what this family spends in comparison to what they earn. How can they do this, and what problems could arise as a result? *The family spends $640 more a month than they earn. They could do this by using credit cards, being behind on their bills, spending other income that's not listed, or by dipping into any savings they may have to make ends meet. They will likely build up too much debt to handle, if they have not already done so.*

What items do you think the family might spend LESS on than what they have budgeted? What budget items, if any, do you think may be too LOW? What might be some estimates that are too LOW? *Answers may vary. Possible over-budgeted items OR under-budgeted items could be miscellaneous household items, entertainment, clothing, doctor visits, medication, etc. These are all categories that can vary widely from month to month.*

List and explain three NEEDS the family must pay for every month. *Answers may include: the mortgage, insurance, food, car payment, gasoline, utilities, etc. These are things the family needs to survive and meet their basic needs.*

List and explain three budget items the family WANTS, but doesn't have to have. *Answers may include: three cell phones PLUS a land line, entertainment, hair and nail care, subscriptions to magazines and newspapers, lessons and activities for the children, gym membership, etc. These all make life more fun or enjoyable but are not necessary to survive.*

Why do you think it's important to distinguish between NEEDS and WANTS in budgeting? Explain. *Answers will vary but should reflect an understanding that if people earn enough money to meet their needs, there may also be enough left over to spend on things they want. However, to get a handle on spending it is important to distinguish between the two in order to make decisions about what MUST be spent and what can be cut.*

What advice would you give this family regarding their financial situation? *Answers may vary but basically, they should cut extras or luxury items, put more money into savings, find cheaper insurance, conserve electricity, water, and gas, etc. Some students may also suggest they seek higher paying jobs to bring in more money per month.*

Do you think making and abiding by a budget is a smart financial habit? Why or why not? *Answers may vary but in general budgets help: get a handle on spending, better account for money and spending, find ways to save, keep track of bills, etc.*

Paying the Bills

Springboard:
Students should complete the "Which is Which?" sorting handout.

Objective: The student will be able to describe the various types of living expenses.

Materials:
Which is Which? (Springboard handout)
In the News (2 page handout)

Terms to know:
living expenses - bills, costs of living
tuition - fees for school or college
utilities - services such as electricity, gas, or water needed for a home
retailer - store or business that sells products and/or services to the public

Procedure:

- While reviewing the Springboard, have the student(s) add examples of their own to each category. Then explain that _this lesson examines three types of expenses that most people have and the relationship between them_.

- Distribute "In the News." Have the student(s) work individually, in pairs, or small groups to analyze the headlines as directed.

- Have the student(s) share their analyses and discuss the following:
  - **?** What are some trends you noticed regarding expenses? (_When people have less money, they generally cut back on their discretionary expenses and vice versa._)
  - **?** What kind of expenses do we have the most of? (_There are more examples of variable expenses but for most people, their fixed expenses account for the largest share of their spending._)
  - **?** Why is it important to distinguish between variable and discretionary expenses? (_Variable expenses tend to be those which we need to live comfortably, while discretionary are those which we could really live without._)
  - **?** Why is it important to understand the differences between living expenses when making a budget? (_We can plan for our fixed expenses because we know they won't change, estimate our variable expenses, and limit discretionary spending._)

- Have the student(s) add lesson examples to their "Assets and Liabilities" organizer. (_Assets could be making sure fixed and variable expenses are paid before discretionary ones, cutting back on discretionary expenses, budgeting for variable expenses, etc. Liabilities might include having high variable or discretionary expenses, which make paying fixed expenses more difficult, etc._)

Which is Which?

DIRECTIONS: Read the descriptions of the three types of expenses. Then list the examples below in the appropriate categories. Be prepared to explain your answers.

Fixed expenses are those bills or costs that don't change from month to month. These tend to be necessary to live. Examples:	**Variable** expenses are bills or costs we pay every month, but the amounts can change based upon our level of use or need. Examples:	**Discretionary** expenses are non-essentials for items we CAN do without. We make a choice to use or purchase these – or not. Examples:

babysitting	newspaper subscription	car oil change
car payment	car insurance	doctor visit
electricity	medicine	haircut
cell phone	veterinary fees	homeowner's insurance
groceries	trash pick up	lawn service
mortgage	student loan payments	charity donation
cable / satellite TV	house cleaning supplies	yard waste pickup
medical insurance	water / sewer service	life insurance
clothing	other utilities	school supplies
movies	gasoline	dry cleaning
school tuition	toothpaste and shampoo	dentist visit
credit card payments	internet service	day care
eating out	concert tickets	furniture
long distance service	laundry soap	parking/tolls

Which is Which? Suggestions for Answers

Fixed expenses are those bills or costs that don't change from month to month. These tend to be necessary to live.

Examples:
- car payment
- mortgage
- medical insurance*
- credit card payments
- car insurance*
- trash pick up
- student loan payments
- homeowner's insurance*
- yard waste pick up
- life insurance*

Student(s) may argue that insurance is not necessary to live, however they should know that homeowner's and car insurance are mandatory.

Variable expenses are bills or costs we pay every month, but the amounts can change based upon our level of use or need.

Examples:
- electricity*
- cell phone*
- groceries
- clothing
- school tuition
- long distance service*
- medicine
- veterinary fees
- house cleaning supplies
- water / sewer service*
- other utilities*
- gasoline
- toothpaste and shampoo
- laundry soap
- car oil change
- doctor visit
- haircut
- school supplies
- dentist visit
- day care
- furniture
- parking / tolls

There may be some question about utilities. Although we can be careful about usage, we must have heat, water, and some means of communication, whereas cable/satellite could be considered luxuries.

Discretionary expenses are non-essentials for items we CAN do without. We make a choice to use or purchase these – or not.

Examples:
- babysitting
- cable / satellite TV
- movies
- eating out
- newspaper subscription
- internet service
- concert tickets
- lawn service
- charity donation
- dry cleaning

These items could all be considered luxury items or things that do not have to be purchased or paid for in order to survive.

In the News

DIRECTIONS: Explain how each headline relates to people's living expenses. Link each to at least one type of expense (fixed, variable, or discretionary) in your explanations.

"Health care costs skyrocket!"
People face overwhelming bills for doctors' visits and medications.

"Gas Prices Provide Relief for Commuters"
AAA reports that gas prices will drop 20 cents a gallon this fall.

"Restaurants on the Ropes!"
Poor economy forcing people to eat in more often.

"Sun and Fun Just Got Cheaper"
Prices for Caribbean vacations and cruises drop dramatically.

"Black Friday Bleak!"
Retailers report huge drop in sales this holiday season.

"Charities Raking it In"

United Way and other charities report donations are at a five year high.

"Tornado Not All Bad News"

Home improvement stores see huge surge in sales after 75% of area homes damaged by the storm.

"Car Dealers Dying Off?"

Dismal economy lead to plummeting auto sales this year.

"Box Office Booming"

Movie theaters see huge ticket sales during economic troubles.

"Doors Closing on Day Care Centers"

Low enrollment forces the closing of five area day care centers.

In the News Suggestions for Answers

NOTE: *Answers may vary, if logical and supported, but suggestions are offered.*

"Health care costs skyrocket!"

Health care can be a fixed (insurance) or variable (doctor visits or medications) expense. An increase in the costs mentioned can therefore increase both fixed and variable expenses as insurance premiums rise with costs. The news will likely bring a drop in discretionary spending.

"Gas Prices Provide Relief for Commuters"

Gasoline is a variable expense, depending on gas prices and usage. When gas prices are down, people have more money for other expenses or may spend the same amounts on gasoline and go out more, carpool less, or forego public transportation.

"Restaurants on the Ropes!"

Eating out at restaurants would be discretionary spending, which people tend to curb in tough times to help meet their fixed and variable expenses. Eating at home saves money and leaves more money for necessities.

"Sun and Fun Just Got Cheaper"

Travel is a discretionary expense people generally undertake when they can meet other expenses first. Lower prices for vacations may entice people to either increase their discretionary spending, cut variable costs to be able to afford travel, or charge the costs and PAY later.

"Black Friday Bleak!"

Holiday gifts are not a necessity, so people spend based on available discretionary funds. If money is tight they will spend less on gifts to have more money for essentials.

"Charities Raking it In"

People will give to charities when they can afford it. Those who donate on a regular basis may consider this a variable expense, and the amount they give will rise or fall depending on how much money they have. Others may only donate to charities once in awhile if they have some discretionary money.

"Tornado Not all Bad News"

Although a tornado or other natural disaster may hurt people financially, if they have insurance (usually a fixed expense), they will get money to fix the damage (a variable expense). They then have money to spend on what normally would be discretionary items to replace damaged ones.

"Car Dealers Dying Off?"

When times are tough, people tend to make do with older cars instead of taking on another fixed expense of a car payment for a new vehicle. This helps pay other fixed and variable expenses.

"Box Office Booming"

Although going out to the movies is a discretionary expense, it is much cheaper than other forms of entertainment. People having trouble meeting other expenses may opt for less expensive entertainment to stretch the discretionary dollars they have.

"Doors Closing on Day Care Centers"

Child care can be a necessary expense (either fixed or variable) for working parents, but becomes discretionary if a person loses his/her job or doesn't make enough to justify the cost.

Bringing Home the Bacon

> **Springboard:**
> Students should complete the "Show Me the Money!" brainstorm handout.
> *(Answers will vary but should reflect an understanding that most of their money as an adult will come from earning income by working.)*

Objective: The student will be able to explain various ways people get "paid."

Materials:
Show Me the Money! (Springboard handout)
Job Offers! (handout)
Job Seekers (handout)

Terms to know:
internship - position that allows someone to learn a profession
benefits - employer-paid insurance, day care, or other costs besides pay
commission - money paid to someone, usually a percentage of sales

Procedure:

- After reviewing the Springboard, explain that *when applying for jobs, there are many things to consider in addition to salary or hourly pay.* Go on to explain that *in this lesson the student(s) will learn about other relevant factors*.

- Distribute "Job Offers!" and review each, making sure the student(s) understand the terms. While discussing each, have the student(s) think of some jobs that might fit these descriptions. *(Answers will vary.)*

- Then distribute the "Job Seekers" handout and have the student(s) work individually, in pairs, or small groups to decide which job offer would be best for each person. *(Answers will vary but should be reasoned and justified.)* **NOTE**: The sample budget on page 22 can be used as reference to help the student(s) better understand the value of having child care, insurance, or car payments as benefits.

- Have the student(s) share their ideas *(Answers may vary but should be well-reasoned.)* and discuss the following:
  - **?** Why do you think employers sometimes offer "perks" such as discounts or cars to potential employees? *(They want to get the best-qualified people for the job. Also, they may have certain enticements available at lesser costs that save money on higher salaries.)*
  - **?** What do you think is the most important thing to consider when looking at job offers? *(Answers will vary.)*

- Have the student(s) add examples from the lesson to the "Assets and Liabilities" organizer. *(An asset would be finding a job with salary, benefits, and perks that meet an individual's needs. Not having sufficient pay or benefits to meet needs would be a liability.)*

SHOW ME THE MONEY!

DIRECTIONS: Brainstorm the various ways that money can be ...

Found:	Won:

Gifted:	Earned:

Where does most of your money come from now? Why?

Where do you think most of your money will come from when you are an adult? Why?

JOB OFFERS!

Offer #1:
- internship
- hourly position
- 30 hours per week including some weekends and evenings
- $20 per hour
- no medical benefits
- access to company gym
- employee discounts for various products such as appliances and clothing
- must commit to a 2-year contract
- opportunity for permanent position with the company after 2 years

What are some possible jobs that fit this description?

Offer #2:
- permanent position
- salary of $45,000 per year ($3750 per month)
- 40 hours per week, no weekends or evenings
- full medical benefits are paid (includes dental and vision care)
- company car is included
- free day care for children under age 5
- company will contribute up to $150 per month in a retirement fund
- 1% raise per year depending on satisfactory performance

What are some possible jobs that fit this description?

Offer #3:
- permanent position
- salary of $100,000 per year ($8333 per month)
- 60-70 hours per week including many early mornings and late nights
- medical benefits are partially paid (approximately ¼ of the cost to be paid by the employee)
- access to company gym
- employee discounts for various products such as appliances and clothing
- opportunity for large bonuses

What are some possible jobs that fit this description?

Offer #4:
- commissioned position with base salary of $20,000 per year ($1666 per month)
- commissions can be as low as $1 and as high as $500,000 per year
- flexible schedule and can work from home
- very frequent travel involved
- no health benefits or other employee perks
- tremendous earning potential; grows each year employee is with the company

What are some possible jobs that fit this description?

JOB SEEKERS

APPLY HERE

DIRECTIONS: Read the profiles and recommend one of the job offers for each person. Make sure you explain your choices!

Job Seeker #1: This job seeker is a 35-year-old parent of four children with a spouse who stays home to care for the two children who are not yet of school age. _____

_____

_____

_____

_____

_____

_____

Job Seeker #2: This 22-year-old recent college graduate lives in a small, inexpensive apartment and has very little debt. _____

_____

_____

_____

_____

_____

_____

Job Seeker #3: This person is a 40-year-old with a spouse who works part time. The couple has two children, one of which has severe asthma that requires medication and frequent trips to the hospital. _____

_____

_____

_____

_____

_____

_____

Job Seeker #4: This job hunter is a 30-year-old single person with mountains of debt from college loans. _____

_____

_____

_____

_____

_____

_____

_____

©InspirEd Educators, Inc.

34

You Can Take That to the Bank!

Springboard:

Students should read "Protecting Your Money?"
and answer the questions.

Objective: The student will be able to explain the purpose of checking accounts.

Materials:
Protecting Your Money? (Springboard handout)
Don't Break the Bank Game board (handout)
Don't ... Bank Game Cards (cut out and shuffled)
Rules/Checking Account Register (handout)
3 coins (2 different coins for pawns and a 3ʳᵈ to flip to move – see below)
Did You Break the Bank? (handout)
calculator or scratch paper for computing

Terms to know:
checking account - bank account that allows money to be easily deposited and withdrawn
deposit - money put into an account
withdraw - money taken out of an account

Procedure:

- After reviewing the Springboard, explain that *people commonly use banks to service their checking accounts*. Go on to explain that *in this lesson the student(s) will play a game to learn about managing personal checking*.

- **For group instruction** have students play the game in pairs. **For individual instruction** the parent/teacher should play the game with the student. Distribute a game board, a set of cards, and three different coins to each pair of players plus a Rules/Register sheet per individual. Explain that *in this game the players will move around the board gaining and spending money. Players take turns flipping a coin to move theirs, one space for heads and two spaces for tails*.

- Review the game materials and rules. (**NOTE:** Depending upon student age and experience, it may be necessary to explain co-pays, ATM's, debit cards, automatic withdrawals, overdraft fees, and online bill paying.)

- When the game is finished, distribute the "Did You Break the Bank?" handout and have the student(s) complete the analysis form.

- Have them share / compare their answers and discuss. (*Answers may vary but should make sense and reflect an understanding of the processes involved in maintaining a check book.*)

- Have the student(s) add examples from this lesson to their "Assets and Liabilities" organizers. (*It would be an asset to regularly keeping track of your checking account with a register or other method so as not to overdraw and to put extra money in a savings account at the end of the month, etc. Liabilities include overdraft fees, overspending, etc.*)

PROTECTING YOUR MONEY?

Depositing money into the first American banks was a risky practice. The first, the Bank of North America, opened in Philadelphia in 1781. This bank and those that followed were not under any sort of government supervision until the National Bank Act of 1865. Before that, they engaged in what was called "wildcat banking." They issued bank notes, or money, that had little or no backing and made more loans than they could afford. These practices led to chaos and confusion, and many people lost their money, as banks closed without being able to give back money that had been deposited.

The Federal Reserve System, established in 1913, sought to put all banking under one central authority, but since most banks were not part of the system, many of the same problems continued and finally came to a head in 1929. When the stock market crashed, signaling the beginning of the Great Depression, people panicked and tried to withdraw their money. But since banks had nowhere near enough cash on hand to cover the withdrawals, 10,000 American banks closed and their customers lost everything.

These events led to major banking reform. The Glass-Steagall Act and the Banking Act were laws passed under President Franklin Roosevelt in hopes of making banks safe for depositors once and for all. The most important outcome of these acts was the creation of the Federal Deposit Insurance Corporation, or FDIC, to instill confidence in bank safety. The FDIC insures deposits up to $100,000. If a bank fails, people can still get their money out up to this amount. When the economy reached near-collapse in 2008, the insured amount was temporarily raised to $250,000 to ease fears until returning to $100,000 in 2014. Besides insuring deposits, the FDIC also oversees banks to keep them strong and __solvent__. It can step in and lend money to those in danger of failure.

The first real test of the FDIC came in the 1980's as laws eased, allowing banks to once more engage in risky loans and other actions that led to widespread failure. Between 1980 and 1988, over five hundred American banks closed, setting off panic and fear among the American people. The agency was again put to the test in 2008, as an economic crisis led to the closing of over one hundred banks in less than two years. However despite the problems, no one lost money due to bank failures, seeming to prove the FDIC does in fact protect bank customers.

The word "solvent" __MOST NEARLY__ means
  A. risky bank practices.
  B. in danger of failing.
  C. having enough money.
  D. not protected by law.

Which sentence __BEST__ states the main idea of the passage?
  A. The FDIC was Roosevelt's most important achievement.
  B. Over time, depositing money in banks has become safer.
  C. The American public tends to panic during hard times.
  D. American banks have had a long and shameful history.

Do you think your money is safer in a bank or in a safe or hiding place at home? Why?

Depositing money into the first American banks was a risky practice. The first, the Bank of North America, opened in Philadelphia in 1781. This bank and those that followed were not under any sort of government supervision until the National Bank Act of 1865. Before that, they engaged in what was called "wildcat banking." They issued bank notes, or money, that had little or no backing and made more loans than they could afford. These practices led to chaos and confusion, and many people lost their money, as banks closed without being able to give back money that had been deposited.

The Federal Reserve System, established in 1913, sought to put all banking under one central authority, but since most banks were not part of the system, many of the same problems continued and finally came to a head in 1929. When the stock market crashed, signaling the beginning of the Great Depression, people panicked and tried to withdraw their money. But since banks had nowhere near enough cash on hand to cover the withdrawals, 10,000 American banks closed and their customers lost everything.

These events led to major banking reform. The Glass-Steagall Act and the Banking Act were laws passed under President Franklin Roosevelt in hopes of making banks safe for depositors once and for all. The most important outcome of these acts was the creation of the Federal Deposit Insurance Corporation, or FDIC, to instill confidence in bank safety. The FDIC insures deposits up to $100,000. If a bank fails, people can still get their money out up to this amount. When the economy reached near-collapse in 2008, the insured amount was temporarily raised to $250,000 to ease fears until returning to $100,000 in 2014. Besides insuring deposits, the FDIC also oversees banks to keep them strong and <u>solvent</u>. It can step in and lend money to those in danger of failure.

The first real test of the FDIC came in the 1980's as laws eased, allowing banks to once more engage in risky loans and other actions that led to widespread failure. Between 1980 and 1988, over five hundred American banks closed, setting off panic and fear among the American people. The agency was again put to the test in 2008, as an economic crisis led to the closing of over one hundred banks in less than two years. However despite the problems, no one lost money due to bank failures, seeming to prove the FDIC does in fact protect bank customers.

The word "solvent" **MOST NEARLY** means

    A. risky bank practices.
    B. in danger of failing.
    C. having enough money. *
    D. not protected by law.
(The FDIC helps banks remain strong and secure with enough money.)

Which sentence **BEST** states the main idea of the passage?

    A. The FDIC was Roosevelt's most important achievement.
    B. Over time, depositing money in banks has become safer. *
    C. The American public tends to panic during hard times.
    D. American banks have had a long and shameful history.
(The passage recounts the history of American banking, highlighting new laws to protect depositors' money and bank stability.)

Do you think your money is safer in a bank or in a safe or hiding place at home? Why?
Answers may vary, but the student(s) should understand that money is INSURED in FDIC banks.

Don't Break the Bank!

Monday	Tuesday	Wednesday	Thursday	Friday	Saturday	Sunday
1 **START** Payday! $1200	2	3 Rent is due! $800 (pay by check)	4	5	6 Internet service bill - due $20 (pay online)	7
8	9 Car insurance - due $80 (automatic debit)	10	11 Student loan payment - due $100 (check)	12	13 Cell phone bill due $50 (pay online)	14
15 Payday! $1200	16	17 Car payment - due $400 (pay by check)	18	19	20 Cable bill - due $75 (pay online)	21
22	23 Gas and electric bills - due $125 (pay online)	24	25 Health insurance - due $100 (automatic debit)	26 Water bill - due $25 (pay online)	27	28 Credit Card payment - due $150 (pay online)
29 Renter's insurance - due $30 (pay by check)	30					

END OF THE MONTH!
Did you break the bank?

Don't Break the Bank - Game Cards

Gas tank on empty! $20 to fill it up on your debit card.	Gas tank on empty! $20 to fill it up on your debit card.	Gas tank on empty! $20 to fill it up on your debit card.	Gas tank on empty! $20 to fill it up on your debit card.
Gas tank on empty! $20 to fill it up on your debit card.	Gas tank on empty! $20 to fill it up on your debit card.	You don't feel like cooking. Will you spend $8 on your debit card for fast food?	You don't feel like cooking. Will you spend $8 on your debit card for fast food?
You don't feel like cooking. Will you spend $8 on your debit card for fast food?	Friends call to go to the movies. Will you spend $20 from the ATM to go?	Shoes on sale! Will you use your debit card to spend $50?	Your friend has a free ticket to a concert. Will you get $50 from the ATM for t-shirts?
You need a haircut for a big meeting at work. You put the $30 on your debit card.	You get the flu and have to see a doctor. Write a check for the $20 co-pay.	You need medicines for the flu. Put the $30 on your debit card.	Your car gets a flat tire. Write a check for the $50 to fix it.
Your parents' anniversary is this weekend. Do you spend $25 on your debit card for a gift?	You're going to a wedding and would love a new outfit. Do you put the $60 outfit on your debit card?	You've run out of laundry supplies. Go to the ATM and get the $15 you need to purchase them.	You are out of toothpaste and shampoo. Use your debit card to purchase $15 worth.
A neighbor's kid is selling candy bars for charity. Do you get $10 from the ATM for one?	Friends call to invite you out to dinner. Do you use your debit card to join them for $25?	You really need new clothes for work. Do you use your debit card to buy $100 worth?	Your texting charges were out of control this month. Pay the $25 overage online.
Friends are coming over to watch the big game. Do you spend $20 on your debit card for snacks?	Your car desperately needs an oil change or it will break down. Write a check for the $30 service.	Your car breaks down. Go to the ATM and use the $30 to take the bus while it's being repaired.	Your refrigerator is empty! Go grocery shopping and spend $75 on your debit card.
Your refrigerator is empty! Go grocery shopping and spend $75 on your debit card.	Your refrigerator is empty! Go grocery shopping and spend $75 on your debit card.	Your refrigerator is empty! Go grocery shopping and spend $75 on your debit card.	Your kitchen sink clogs up. Write a check to the plumber for $60 to fix it.
Go to the hardware store to buy supplies to fix your leaky sink. Put the $50 on your debit card.	Do you buy a subscription to your favorite magazine? If the answer is yes, write a check for $25.	You're really bored on a Friday night. Do you go rent movies for $15? If yes, put it on your debit card.	Your computer crashes again! You can upgrade your memory for $100 on your debit card.
Your best friend's birthday is tomorrow. Do you buy a gift? If so, put $25 on your debit card.	Your coffee maker breaks but Starbuck's is $5 a cup! Buy a new machine on your debit card for $30.	You're out of trash bags and cleaning supplies. Put the $30 on your debit card.	The friend you borrowed money from wants to be paid back NOW! Write a check for $40.

Rules of the Game

1. You will start your "month" with the first of two paydays. Enter the credit on your register in the appropriate column. You will not get another credit until your second payday.
2. As you move along the board, you will either land on spaces with "fixed" expenses (which you need to debit from your account) or $ spaces. If you do not land on them, you must pay them as you pass.
3. If you land on a $ space, pick a card. If given a choice to spend the money, announce your decision and deduct the amount from your account if you decide to do so. Many cards do not offer a choice; you must deduct the stated amount from your register to keep up with your checking account.
4. If at any time your balance is less than zero, you must pay a $25 OVERDRAFT FEE to your bank and make the deduction on your register. If you continue to make purchases before being paid, you must pay a $25 OVERDRAFT FEE for each expense or purchase.
5. At the end of the game, the person with the highest balance wins.

Checking Account Register

DIRECTIONS: Use this chart to keep track of all your credits and debits during the game Make sure you record the date, how the payment was made (automatic debit, ATM, check, etc.), a description of what was paid for, and the running balance of your checking account.

Date	Method of payment	Description	Debit	Credit	Balance

Did You Break the Bank?

1. Did you have enough money as you went through the month? Why or why not?

2. Describe any trends you saw in your balance throughout the month.

3. Did you incur any overdraft fees? Why? How would these fees affect your budget?

4. Why do you think it is important to keep a checking account register?

5. What purchase decisions were choices, and what spending was mandatory during the game?

6. What are the advantages of the different types of payments (cash, debit cards, etc.) made from checking accounts? What are some disadvantages of each?

7. Are checking accounts convenient? Why or why not?

8. If you had money left at the end of the game, what do you think you should do with it?

9. How would your strategy have changed if you received all of your pay for the month at one time? Why?

10. What did you learn about managing money from playing this game?

1. Did you have enough money as you went through the month? Why or why not? *Answers will vary. Players that ran out of money likely ran into a lot of unexpected mandatory expenses (such as car repair, illness, etc.) or decided to make extra purchases.*

2. Describe any trends you saw in your balance throughout the month. *Answers will vary, but students should see that checking account balances go up or down, depending upon the point in a person's pay cycle and bill paying. Usually by the end of the month or pay cycle, there isn't much money in a checking account.*

3. Did you incur any overdraft fees? Why? How can these fees affect your budget for the month? *Answers will vary, but students who incurred overdraft fees didn't have enough money in their account to pay for bills or purchases. They should see that these fees can ADD UP QUICKLY and become a major monthly expense if a checkbook is kept carelessly.*

4. Why do you think it is important to keep a checking account register? *A register allows the account holder to document spending (much like a budget) and keep track of his/her balance to avoid overdraft fees!*

5. What purchase decisions were choices, and what spending was mandatory during the game? *Choices involved spending for entertainment, gifts, or extra clothing or shoes. Illnesses, car, or home repairs, and supplies like gasoline, food, and other household items arise frequently, whether a person has money to pay for them or not!*

6. What are the advantages of the different types of payments (cash, debit cards, etc.) made from checking accounts? What are some disadvantages of each? *Answers may vary. Debit cards, on-line bill paying, and automatic withdrawals are very convenient, but must be accounted for. Checks and cash (ATM's) are sometimes required if a place of business cannot take a debit card.*

7. Are checking accounts convenient? Why or why not? *Answers will vary, but students are likely to see them as convenient, as there are many ways to withdrawal money for a variety of needs.*

8. If you had money left at the end of the game, what do you think you should do with it? *Answers will vary, but if not mentioned, suggest that putting the money into a savings account is a smart financial move. Savings can help when unforeseen situations arise; illness, loss of job, home or auto repairs, etc.*

9. How would your strategy have changed if you received all of your pay for the month at one time? Why? *Answers may vary, but note that more care should have been taken with spending to make money last.*

10. What did you learn about managing money from playing this game? *Answers will vary but should spark discussion.*

Getting A Deal

Springboard:

Students should complete "What's the Message?"
(The sayings are warning people to be smart consumers.)

Objective: The student will be able to describe several types of deceptive advertising that can trick or harm consumers.

Materials:

What's the Message? (Springboard handout)
Buyer Beware! (2 page handout)
Smart Shoppers (handout and alternate rubric – see note below)

Terms to know:

consumer - someone buying goods or services
deceptive - misleading, not as it seems
endorse - to approve of; vouch for or recommend

Procedure:

· After reviewing the Springboard, explain that *in this lesson student(s) will learn more about being smart consumers* (*review term*).

· Distribute the "Buyer Beware! handouts and have the student(s) complete it individually or in pairs.

· Lead a discussion of their ideas to ensure understanding of the various types of illegal advertising.

· Distribute the "Smart Shoppers" guidelines and rubric and review the directions. **For group instruction** the students should work in groups of three or four to complete the project. **For individualized instruction** the student should choose at least one of the mediums described.

· Then have them share and evaluate their work. (**NOTE:** An alternate rubric is provided for individual projects.)

· Have the student(s) add lesson examples to the "Assets and Liabilities" organizer. (*Assets include careful examination of advertisements, reporting violations of advertising laws, etc. Liabilities would be getting "taken" by false advertising, not researching purchases, etc.*)

WHAT'S THE MESSAGE?

If it seems too good to be true, it probably is.

There's no such thing as a free lunch.

You get what you pay for.

What do you think these sayings all have in common? Explain the "message" in your own words. _____

_____

_____

_____

_____

Give a real-life example that demonstrates this message. _____

_____

_____

_____

Do you have any personal experience with this message? What happened to you? _____

_____

_____

_____

_____

_____

_____

How does understanding this message make you a smarter shopper?_____

_____

_____

_____

_____

_____

BUYER BEWARE!

DIRECTIONS: Read the descriptions of some of the ways consumers can be deceived by advertisements. For each type of deceptive advertising, jot down an ad or commercial you have seen, or think of an example of your own of an advertisement that fits the description. Then briefly explain how these tactics hurt consumers.

Bait and switch: These advertisements are meant to lure customers in with an offer or sale on something the seller either doesn't stock and claims they're out of or never meant to sell in the first place. Once they have a buyer in the store, they try to sell something else, usually a "better," though more expensive item.

Misleading endorsements: We often see celebrities endorse products, most of which they have rarely if ever used. Many people admire and even want to be like celebrities, and might be swayed to buy something they mistakenly believe the star uses and highly recommends.

Deceptive sale pricing: A "sale" MUST BE a reduction in the regular price. A retailer cannot raise a price, and then turn around and put the item "on sale." Yet this is a common method of getting people into stores to buy things.

Buy one get one free: A seller cannot double or otherwise raise the price of an item and then give one away for "free" to lure customers into the store! Of course some do.

Hidden fees and surcharges: Retailers often advertise what seems like a low price, but may not include shipping and handling, annual fees, user fees, etc. The seller SHOULD make any extra charges known, but they often do so in such small print or confusing wording that the buyer easily misses the message.

Free trials: Sellers sometimes offer a service or product free for a certain amount of time. Then once that period ends, the buyer is charged without any further communication or warning. The charges may show up as credit card charges or account debits, which the consumer may not even notice.

False "sales": Retailers might advertise that they are going out of business and offer all stock at half off or more. This practice can be deceptive in one of two ways: first the store may not be going out of business at all, but new products are being brought in daily for the big "sale." In other situations the products are labeled with much higher prices and then "discounted."

Misleading photographs: Sellers might show "before" and "after" pictures to advertise the effectiveness of products. Yet photographs can be easily touched up with computer programs to make results look amazing! Also, pictures often make the product look better than it actually is.

Scare tactics: Sellers might use advertising to instill fear, uncertainty, or doubt to spur consumers to act to protect themselves and all they hold dear!

SMART SHOPPERS

For this assignment you will design and create advertisements to illustrate deceptive practices. You should pick four types of deceptive advertising from the "Buyer Beware!" handout and find or create ads as follows:

- A written classified advertisement
- A pictorial advertisement that could be displayed in a flyer, newspaper, magazine, or store window
- A script for a commercial, including characters, action, and dialogue
- An actual advertisement found in a newspaper, circular, or other source with a written explanation of how it fits one type of deceptive advertising

For group work, tasks should be delegated among group members, who should work as a team to complete all four elements of the assignment. Make sure your work clearly illustrates the type of deceptive advertisement and that your work is NEAT and CREATIVE!

- -

SMART SHOPPERS GROUP SCORING GUIDE

My contributions to the assignment: _____

_____

_____

_____

Evaluate your work using the following scale:

0 - Unacceptable	2 - Fair	4 - Excellent
1 - Poor	3 - Good	

Category	Student	Teacher
Clear depiction of concept	_____	_____
Four types represented	_____	_____
Four types of ads complete	_____	_____
Creativity	_____	_____
Writing mechanics	_____	_____

Overall Score/Grade:

Comments:

SMART SHOPPERS INDIVIDUAL SCORING GUIDE

Evaluate your work using the following scale:

0 - Unacceptable   2 - Fair   4 - Excellent
1 - Poor   3 - Good

Category	Student	Teacher
Clear depiction of concept(s)	_____	_____
Appropriate number of ads created	_____	_____
Assigned types of ads complete	_____	_____
Creativity	_____	_____
Writing mechanics	_____	_____

Grade:

Comments:

What did you do BEST on this assignment? Why? _____

_____

_____

_____

_____

What do you think you could have done BETTER? Why? _____

_____

_____

_____

_____

What did you learn from doing this assignment? _____

_____

_____

_____

_____

_____

Paying with Plastic

> **Springboard:**
>
> Students should study the "Kids and Credit" statistics
> and answer the questions. (*Answers will vary; trends could include
> more young people using credit, accumulating debt, etc.*)

Objective: The student will be able to explain the dangers of using credit cards.

Materials: Kids and Credit (Springboard handout)
Studying a Statement (2-page handout)
Cash or Credit? (handout)

Terms to know: **credit** - buying something to be paid for later
interest - a charge for borrowing money (also money earned on deposits)
statement - itemized list of a customer's account information

Procedure:

- After reviewing the Springboard, explain that *in this lesson the student(s) will learn more about using credit cards.*
- Distribute "Studying a Statement" and explain that *a consumer who uses a credit card receives a statement listing the amount due, payment terms, and other information each month.* The student(s) should work individually or in pairs to conduct Internet research to learn the meaning of each term and complete the handout. (**NOTE:** A search for "understanding a credit card statement" nets good results. There are many websites written in layman's terms to explain the topic.)
- Have the student(s) share / compare answers, adding additional information as appropriate.
- Then distribute "Cash or Credit?" The student(s) should complete the analysis form based on their research and their own ideas.
- Have them share their answers and discuss. During the discussion, refer back to the Springboard asking how the student(s)' views about the use of credit cards may have changed as a result of what they have learned.
- Have them add examples from the lesson to their "Assets and Liabilities" organizer. (*Assets include using cash as much as possible, keeping credit card debt to a minimum, etc. Liabilities would be too much credit card debt, late payments on credit cards, etc.*)

Kids and Credit

DIRECTIONS: Study the statistics regarding young people and credit cards. Then answer the questions that follow.

One in three high school seniors use credit cards. About half of these have a credit card in their own name. (Source: JumpStart Coalition for Personal Financial Literacy)

Fifty four percent of college freshmen carry a credit card. College freshmen average $1585 in credit card debt. 92% of college sophomores carry a credit card. (Source: The Nellie Mae Corporation)

The number of college freshmen with credit cards tripled between 1999 and 2002. Between 7 and 10% of college students drop out due to too much credit card debt. (Source: Manning, Robert. Credit Card Nation: The Consequences of America's Addiction to Credit)

Most teenagers (51%) think it's easier to pay with a credit card than cash.

Nearly one in three teens would rather use a credit card than cash.

Twenty nine percent of teenagers already have credit card debt.

Only 30% of teens think their parents are concerned about teaching them money management.

Only 24% of teens say they have been taught to use credit cards responsibly.

One fourth of teenagers say their parents are more likely to use a credit card than cash. (Source: Teens and Money 2007 survey reports, Charles Schwab Brokerage Firm)

What trends do you notice regarding these statistics?

What do you think these statistics say about the way young people view money?

Do you see these findings as a problem? Why or why not?

What are your views regarding the use of credit cards?

STUDYING A STATEMENT

DIRECTIONS: Use the Internet to find out what these terms and provisions about credit mean. Jot a short explanation and briefly explain why it is important for consumers to understand how these work.

current balance -

billing cycle -

statement closing date -

purchases / new charges -

previous balance -

payments / credits -

cash advance -

finance charges -

APR -

STUDYING A STATEMENT

average daily balance -

grace period -

minimum payment -

due date -

credit limit -

late fee -

over the limit fee -

annual fee -

cash advance fee -

lost or stolen card procedures -

STUDYING A STATEMENT - SUGGESTIONS FOR ANSWERS

NOTE: *Basic information is provided. Opinions on the importance may vary.*

current balance - *the total amount of money owed to the credit card company, not including charges made since the end of the last statement period*

billing cycle - *the period of time (usually around 30 days) a statement covers*

statement closing date - *the last day of the billing cycle; the last day charges will be included in that month's statement*

purchases / new charges - *the purchases made or cash advances taken since the last statement; credit card users are advised to keep receipts to check against the statement*

previous balance - *amount owed on the previous statement*

payments / credits - *what was paid since the last statement; can also include credits for returned items for which receipts and records should be kept to check for accuracy*

cash advances - *cash borrowed from a credit card (Higher-than-normal finance charges or special fees are often charged for such transactions.)*

finance charges - *the amount of money paid in interest each month; whatever amount paid each month is applied to the finance charges before coming off the balance*

APR - *the "annual percentage rate" or percentage the borrower is charged in interest on his/her balance; different companies charge different APR's and these can change from month to month (Consumers should monitor statements for changes!)*

average daily balance - *usually used to calculate the amount of interest; the balance is added up and divided by the number of days to find the average*

grace period - *the amount of time the company allows to pay off a balance before charging interest; doesn't apply to balances carried from month to month*

minimum payment - *the lowest payment the company will allow for a month; usually around 2% of your balance. (It can take a long time to pay off a balance with the minimum payment each month since it barely covers the interest!)*

due date - *the day that a payment must be RECORDED (not mailed, received, or postmarked) to be considered on time and to avoid late payment fees*

credit limit - *This is the most money you are allowed to purchase or borrow. If you pay your card late, the company can lower the amount.*

late fee - *what the company charges for paying after the due date (average fee is $30!)*

over the limit fee - *what the company charges for going over the stated limit in purchases or if other fees take you over your limit. (Rather than decline charges, some companies LOVE consumers to exceed their credit limit!)*

annual fee - *fee charged by some companies to be paid each year for use of their card*

cash advance fee - *a charge for borrowing money from a credit card; can be a flat fee or a percentage of the amount of cash received*

lost or stolen card procedures - *lost or stolen cards must be reported immediately (Some companies hold consumers responsible for everything charged by a thief before the lost or stolen card is reported! However, if a family member uses a card without permission, credit card holders must take court action to be released from the charges!)*

CA$H OR CREDIT?

Advantages of using credit cards	Disadvantages of using credit cards

Under what circumstances do you think credit cards can or should be used? _____

_____

_____

_____

_____

Under what circumstances do you think credit cards should NOT be used?

_____

_____

_____

_____

_____

Explain four precautions that should be taken when using credit cards:

1.

2.

3.

4.

CA$H OR CREDIT?
$UGGESTION$ FOR ANSWER$

Advantages of using credit cards	Disadvantages of using credit cards
• *May be safer to carry than cash* • *Can establish credit if used wisely* • *Can be used in an emergency* • *Can be used for things needed right away when cash is not available*	• *Can lead to credit problems* • *Can lead to overspending* • *Can result in impulse buys* • *Fees and interest can make paying off a balance very difficult and take a long time* • *Can be lost or stolen, leading to charges* • *Items purchased are not "owned" for a long time* • *Stiff fees charged for a variety of items and services*

Under what circumstances do you think credit cards can or should be used? *Answers may vary. Student(s) may argued that there are appropriate times to use credit cards (emergencies, controlled shopping, etc.), but efforts should be made to pay off balances as soon as possible to avoid interest and other fees. The student(s) may give examples of their parents using cards for expense accounts or other situations where they are convenient, but not to overspend what one can afford.*

Under what circumstances do you think credit cards should NOT be used? *Answers may vary but should reflect an understanding that it's not a good idea to use them to purchase things that are not affordable and cannot be paid off. Rampant spending results in debt that can take a long time to pay off due to high interest and fees.*

Explain four precautions that should be taken when using credit cards:
Answers will vary but could include:
• *Read terms and statements carefully to know when payments are due and what interest will be charged.*
• *Pay more than the minimum balance every month!*
• *Research credit card companies for lower fees, no annual fees, etc.*
• *Pay off the balance to avoid interest fees.*
• *Do not assume if your card is accepted that you are not over your limit.*
• *Keep credit cards safe and have the necessary information recorded somewhere accessible in case a card has to be reported lost or stolen.*
• *Keep receipts to compare to statement. It cannot be automatically assumed that the credit card company's records are accurate; and some can be misleading.*

Reporting In

> **Springboard:**
> Students should read "Keeping Score" and answer the questions.

Objective: The student will be able to explain what can raise and lower credit ratings and why they are important.

Materials: Keeping Score (Springboard handout)
                   Credit Report Roundup (2-page handout)

Terms to know: **credit rating** - an evaluation of a person's ability to pay their bills and debts
                 credit score - a three digit number used to summarize one's financial borrowing and repayment history
                 credit report - a statement of a person's borrowing and repaying history
                 bankruptcy - a court proceeding for a person who is unable to pay debts to settle with those owed money

Procedure:

- After reviewing the Springboard, explain that *in addition to looking at credit scores, lenders also use credit reports* (see term) *to decide whether or not to lend someone money*. Go on to explain that *in this lesson the student(s) will examine a credit report to learn what it includes and what can raise or lower one's overall score*.

- Distribute the "Credit Report Roundup" and have the student(s) work individually or in pairs to analyze the report as instructed, adding their ideas about what can help or hurt to each section.

- Have the student(s) share / compare their ideas. (*Answers may vary, but in general credit ratings are higher when people pay their bills on time, have stable employment and residence, and don't have too much debt or "open" or available credit. Ratings are lower when people bounce from job to job or residence to residence, pay bills late or not at all, declare bankruptcy, or have court judgments against them, such as having to pay child support or other court-required payments.*) Additional Teacher information is provided to help spark discussion. Include the following questions in discussion:
  - **?** What are some future situations in which your credit report or rating could be a factor? (*Credit scores affect buying a house, renting an apartment, buying a car, being granted student or other loans, etc.*)
  - **?** Why is it important for you to have good financial habits, starting now? (*Bad decisions can come back to haunt you for many years after!*)

- Have student(s) add examples to their organizers. (*Assets include monitoring one's credit report for errors. Liabilities could be any actions that lower ratings, etc.*)

KEEPING SCORE

A credit score is a number used by lenders such as banks and other financial institutions to decide whether or not to loan money or extend credit to someone. This number can range from 300 to a perfect 850. The formula used to determine this number was developed by The Fair Isaac Corporation, also known as FICO, a credit bureau established in 1956. A variety of information is used to determine one's credit score, but the final number gives creditors an easy way to make decisions as to whether or not someone is a good risk.

A good credit score not only helps people get loans, but can also determine the rate of interest that will be charged on that loan. The best interest rates are usually only offered to people who have solid credit history. In recent years, credit scores have also been used by insurance companies. Studies for this industry show that people who are in debt or have poor financial habits are more likely to make insurance claims. Therefore people with low credit scores may have to pay higher prices for automobile and homeowner's insurance. Although the formula used to determine credit scores is not public information, the number breaks down approximately as follows:

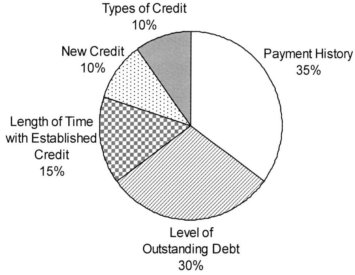

Which of these statements is **NOT** supported by passage information?
   A. A credit score of four hundred is poor.
   B. A poor credit score can cost you money.
   C. Your credit score can never be changed.
   D. You cannot figure your own credit score.

According to the graphic, it is **MOST** important to
   A. always pay your bills by the due date.
   B. have many different types of credit.
   C. establish credit as young as possible.
   D. limit the amount of credit you have.

Which word **BEST** describes one's credit score?
   A. usual   B. habitual   C. influential   C. lending

A credit score is a number used by lenders such as banks and other financial institutions to decide whether or not to loan money or extend credit to someone. This number can range from 300 to a perfect 850. The formula used to determine this number was developed by The Fair Isaac Corporation, also known as FICO, a credit bureau established in 1956. A variety of information is used to determine one's credit score, but the final number gives creditors an easy way to make decisions as to whether or not someone is a good risk.

A good credit score not only helps people get loans, but can also determine the rate of interest that will be charged on that loan. The best interest rates are usually only offered to people who have solid credit history. In recent years, credit scores have also been used by insurance companies. Studies for this industry show that people who are in debt or have poor financial habits are more likely to make insurance claims. Therefore people with low credit scores may have to pay higher prices for automobile and homeowner's insurance. Although the formula used to determine credit scores is not public information, the number breaks down approximately as follows:

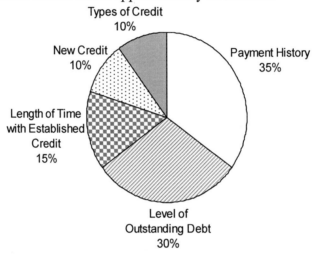

Which of these statements is **NOT** supported by passage information?
   A. A credit score of four hundred is poor.
   B. A poor credit score can cost you money.
   C. Your credit score can never be changed. *
   D. You cannot figure your own credit score.
   (The passage does not mention changing scores, but it can be inferred that the score WOULD go up or down with one's credit situation at any given time.)

According to the graphic, it is **MOST** important to
   A. always pay your bills by the due date. *
   B. have many different types of credit.
   C. establish credit as young as possible.
   D. limit the amount of credit you have.
   (Since payment history makes up about 35% of the credit score, that would be the MOST important factor.)

Which word **BEST** describes one's credit score?
   A. usual   B. habitual   C. influential*   C. lending
   (The main point of the passage is how influential one's credit score is to many aspects of life: buying a home, car, getting loans, or even buying insurance.)

Credit Report Roundup

DIRECTIONS: Study the credit report contents. In the space provided jot ideas about what you think could help or hurt one's credit rating and why this type of information is helpful to a lender.

Your Notes:

Section I: Identification
A. Name
B. Current address
C. Social Security number
D. Date of birth
E. Spouse's name (if applicable)

Section II: Credit History
A. List of open and past credit accounts
    1. Includes debts that have not been paid off as well as those accounts that are paid off
    2. Any late payments are listed

B. Basic format is listed as follows:
    1. Company name - company reporting the information
    2. Account number - of the account
    3. Whose account - who took out the loan or account
        a. Individual
        b. Joint (with another person: parent, spouse, etc.)
    4. Date opened
    5. Months reviewed - amount of time the account was reported
    6. Last activity - could be last payment or date the account was closed
    7. High credit - the highest amount that was borrowed or charged
    8. Terms - only for installment loans (those that have a fixed number of payments)
    9. Balance - "zero" if paid off; other amount if not
    10. Past due - any amounts late or past due
    11. Status - type of account (installment, open – as a credit card, etc.)

Section III: Collection Accounts
A. This section lists any accounts that have been reported to collections agencies
    1. Occurs when a creditor cannot collect money owed
    2. A collection agency works for a fee to pursue payments

Your Notes:

Section IV: Courthouse Records
A. Also referred to as "public records"
B. Can come from local, state or federal court systems
C. Includes any or all of the following:
    1. Bankruptcy records
        a. Occurs when someone cannot pay their debts
        b. Asks a judge for protection from collections
    2. Tax liens
        a. Creditors can place a "hold" on someone's property such as home or automobile.
        b. When that property is sold, the creditor gets paid what is owed to them first
    3. Judgments
        a. Money one may have to pay if sued
        b. Any such money due is recorded here
    4. Collections accounts that have gone to court
    5. Overdue child support or other obligations

Section V: Other Information
A. Past addresses and employers
    1. Creditors add this information to the file
    2. Gives other creditors assistance in collecting debts

Section VI: Inquiry Section
A. This section lists businesses that have requested a copy of the person's credit report
B. Information remains for previous 24 months

Miscellaneous information regarding credit reports:
- Credit and collection information can only be reported for seven years from the date of the last activity
- Bankruptcy information can only be reported for 10 years from the date bankruptcy is filed
- A creditor can only get a copy of a person's credit report with that person's permission
- If incorrect information shows up on a credit report, a "dispute letter" can be written that appears on the report

In general what do you think you can you do NOW to ensure that your credit report is good in the future? _____

_____

_____

_____

_____

Credit Report Information - Suggested Notes

NOTE: *Although student ideas may vary widely, the following information regarding credit reports can help spark discussion:*

Section I: Identification

- *This information helps creditors identify the person they are considering for a loan.*

- *When reviewing one's credit report, it is important to make sure this information is correct. For example if one digit of the Social Security number is off, the financial information for an entirely different person could be examined.*

Section II: Credit History

- *This is the "meat" of the report that creditors find MOST relevant. It paints a picture of the financial habits of a potential customer; paying bills late or not at all make a person look like a very bad risk to creditors.*

- *However, having several accounts that have been paid on time and in full make the person look like a good risk, presenting a history of responsibility.*

Section III: Collections Accounts

- *Having accounts referred to collections agencies can greatly harm one's credit rating. It basically says to a potential creditor that the person refused to pay bills at the request of the company that extended him/her credit.*

- *Collections agencies use many methods to collect debts. They make constant phone calls demanding payments and send letters threatening further action. Although collections agencies do not have the power to bring lawsuits, they often collect money by harassing and intimidating people.*

- *Creditors use collections agencies only after they are unable to collect the debt themselves. They pay the agencies a portion of the money collected or a flat fee.*

Section IV: Courthouse Records

- *Although some of these categories can be complicated, the student(s) should understand that bankruptcies, liens, and collections judgments are very serious and can greatly affect a one's credit rating for much longer than late payments.*

Section V: Additional Information

- *Many addresses or frequently switching employers can make a person look unstable.*

- *Additionally the student(s) should understand that credit companies often provide information to help other companies collect their debts, too.*

Section VI: Inquiry Section

- *It can look bad to creditors to have too many inquiries; they may assume the person is trying to open many accounts to have access to more credit than they can afford, or that they have been turned down by many other creditors.*

Miscellaneous Information:

- *The student(s) should understand that poor financial decisions and irresponsible behavior in terms of credit can haunt them for a very long time!*

Buddy, Can You Spare a Dime?

Springboard:
Students should complete "The Lowdown on Loans" handout.

Objective: The student will be able to explain how loans work and describe what is involved in getting a loan.

Materials:
The Lowdown on Loans (Springboard handout)
It's Your Job to Decide (cut out cards)
Application Review (1/2-sheet handout)

Terms to know:
loan officer - person who reviews and makes decisions about loan applications
down payment - money paid towards a purchase that does not need to be borrowed
closing costs - loan fees and other costs for borrowing money (in addition to interest)

Procedure:

· After reviewing the Springboard, explain that *in this lesson the student(s) will take on the role of a loan officer*.

· **For group instruction** arrange the students into eight groups, giving each one "It's Your Job to Decide" card and an "Application Review." Groups should read their scenarios, discuss, and complete the review. **For individual instruction** the student can examine as many scenarios as desired, completing a review for each.

· Have the student(s) share their decisions and advice and discuss the following questions:

? What factor(s) did you take into consideration when making your decisions? *(Answers may vary, but students should apply what was learned about good and bad credit ratings from the last lesson.)*

? How do credit ratings make a loan officer's job easier? How do they make it harder? *(Answers will vary. Credit ratings take personal circumstances such as hardship out of the picture, making decisions more objective. However, people who may need loans can't get them because of bad financial decisions in the past or some circumstances out of their control.)*

? Do you think knowing how to apply for and get loans will help you in the future? *(Answers may vary, but since most people have to apply for some sort of loan at some point in their lifetime, preparing for and understanding the process should be very helpful!)*

· Have the student(s) add examples to the "Assets and Liabilities" organizer. *(Assets would include paying off loans early, getting lower interest rates, and putting money down to make loans "cheaper," etc. Liabilities could include costly loans with high interest rates, no down payments, making poor decisions that make loans harder to get, etc.)*

The Lowdown on Loans

If you are buying a home for $100,000, here are options to consider: *

Borrow the entire cost of the home at 7% interest for 30 years:
  monthly payment = $665.30
  total cost of loan = $239,508

Put a down payment of $15,000 at 7% interest for 30 years:
  monthly payment = $565.51
  total cost of the loan = $203,454

You have average credit so your interest rate is 8% for 30 years:
  monthly payment = $773.76
  total cost of the loan = $278,553

You have excellent credit so your interest rate is 6% for 30 years:
  monthly payment = $599.55
  total cost of the loan = $215,838

You take out a shorter loan period of 20 years at 7% interest:
  monthly payment = $775.30
  total cost of the loan = $186,072

*   These options do not include other costs for a mortgage. These can be paid separately or added to the amount of money you borrow:
   2009 National Average for closing costs = $2748.00
   (Includes points, application fees, document preparation fees, lender fees, appraisal fees, inspection fees, title insurance, processing fees, underwriter fees, and others)

1. What kinds of things should we consider when taking out loans? Why?

2. What other kinds of things do people need loans for?

3. Who needs loans? Who doesn't?

4. Do you think getting a loan is easy? Why or why not?

5. Do you think closing costs should be an important consideration when making loan decisions? Why or why not?

If you are buying a home for $100,000, here are options to consider: *

Borrow the entire cost of the home at 7% interest for 30 years:
> monthly payment = $665.30
> total cost of loan = $239,508

Put a down payment of $15,000 at 7% interest for 30 years:
> monthly payment = $565.51
> total cost of the loan = $203,454

You have average credit so your interest rate is 8% for 30 years:
> monthly payment = $773.76
> total cost of the loan = $278,553

You have excellent credit so your interest rate is 6% for 30 years:
> monthly payment = $599.55
> total cost of the loan = $215,838

You take out a shorter loan period of 20 years at 7% interest:
> monthly payment = $775.30
> total cost of the loan = $186,072

* These options do not include other costs for a mortgage. These can be paid separately or added to the amount of money you borrow:
2009 National Average for closing costs = $2748.00
(Includes points, application fees, document preparation fees, lender fees, appraisal fees, inspection fees, title insurance, processing fees, underwriter fees, and others)

1. What kinds of things should we consider when taking out loans? Why? *In general factors to consider include: the total cost of the loan; how much money is required down; and lower terms and interest rates will save money in the long run. For example a $100,000 home at the longest term with no money down at the highest interest rate would end up almost tripling the cost of the home to $278,553!*

2. What other kinds of things do people need loans for? *Answers may vary: automobiles, boats, motorcycles, school (student loans), home improvement, furniture, appliances, electronics, etc. are all possibilities.*

3. Who needs loans? Who doesn't? *Answers may vary, but almost EVERYONE will take out a loan at some point! The only people who may never need loans are those who are extremely rich and have A LOT of cash!*

4. Do you think getting a loan is easy? Why or why not? *Answers will vary. Generally higher loan amounts are harder to get than smaller loans. Also, a good credit score makes it MUCH easier to get loans.*

5. Do you think closing costs should be an important consideration when making loan decisions? Why or why not? *Closing costs should be taken into account because they can be expensive! If costs are "rolled into" a loan, it can raise a monthly payment significantly! (NOTE: It is not necessary for students to be able to define each type of cost. The intent is simply for them to see that there are A LOT of costs associated with loans.)*

It's Your Job to Decide

A forty-year-old man with four children recently lost his wife from injuries she received in a car accident. He has come to you for a $25,000 loan to buy a new van for his family. His credit rating is average, but recently his hours at work have been cut due to the slow economy. He received enough life insurance when his wife died to pay off his home loan but still has thousands of dollars of debt from medical bills resulting from the accident that his health insurance did not pay. Now that his wife is gone, he will need to hire a nanny or other child care for the youngest two children who are not yet in school.

A twenty-seven-year-old couple has come to you for a loan so they can purchase their first home. They want to take out a mortgage for $125,000 to buy a $140,000 home. Once they make their $15,000 down payment, they will have nothing in their savings account. The wife has excellent credit and brought very little debt to the marriage. The husband, however, has a number of late payments on his credit report and still owes thousands of dollars in student loans from college. Both have good jobs but have only been employed by their companies for about six months.

A single, thirty-year-old business owner wants a business loan of $50,000 to buy new computer equipment, pay for advertising, and redecorate her office to look more successful as a means of attracting clients. Her company has made great strides over the last year, allowing her to take a salary of over $100,000 this year. However, the year before she only made $15,000 salary and as a result, racked up $35,000 in credit card debt to pay her living expenses while her business was getting started. She was also late a couple of times on her bills during that tough first year.

A fifty-year-old man wants to borrow $80,000 to buy a condominium. He has been living in a rented apartment for the last five years, always paying his rent on time. However, five years ago he had to declare bankruptcy due to a messy divorce that cost him thousands of dollars he could not afford to pay back when he lost his job. Since that time, he has been steadily employed, used no credit cards, and has met all of the requirements ordered by the bankruptcy judge in his case. He has no money to put down on the purchase of his new home and has no savings.

A seventy-year-old retired couple wants to borrow $40,000 to buy a new Cadillac. The two have hundreds of thousands of dollars in savings and no bills other than the monthly rent and utilities they pay to the retirement community where they live. However, both have grown forgetful in recent years and so have been late on their bills every month. It has happened so often that the retirement community has threatened to evict them if they don't start paying on time! The couple has not had any credit history for many years, as they paid off their home twenty years ago and don't use credit cards.

A thirty-year-old woman comes to you to borrow $200,000 for a new home. She has lived in six different apartments and has held five different jobs since she graduated from college eight years ago. Right now, she has a great job and makes an excellent salary, but she has only been employed by her company for six weeks. Her credit is good overall, though she has paid her credit card bill late a couple of times. She does not have any savings for a down payment, and when you run a credit check, you see that there have been several other requests for her credit report in recent months.

A twenty-one-year-old man comes to you for a personal loan. He wants to go to graduate school but cannot get a student loan because his credit score is extremely low. He took out several credit cards while in college and charged them all to the limit. Then when he couldn't pay the balances, several of the accounts were sent to collections. His parents have co-signed for him to get a car and an apartment, but they refuse to help him anymore. They think he should work for a few years to pay off his debt, and then go to graduate school to further his career.

An eighteen-year-old woman comes to you for a car loan. She wants $10,000 to buy a reliable used vehicle which she desperately needs to get to work. Her parents kicked her out of the house when she dropped out of high school, but she has managed to secure a cheap apartment and a minimum wage job. The problem she's having is there is no public transportation for her to get to and from work. She has no credit history at all and was only able to get the apartment because the landlord felt sorry for her. She has no money to put down and has only lived on her own for a month.

Application Review

Application is: Approved _____   Denied _____

Explain the reasons for your decision. _____

_____

_____

_____

_____

_____

What financial advice would you give this person for the future? _____

_____

_____

_____

_____

Application Review

Application is: Approved _____   Denied _____

Explain the reasons for your decision. _____

_____

_____

_____

_____

_____

What financial advice would you give this person for the future? _____

_____

_____

_____

_____

"Taken"

Objective: Students will be able to describe identity theft and explain how to avoid it.

Materials: David's Story (Springboard handout)
                              Financial News Hour (4-page handout)
                              What to Know, What to Do (handout)

Terms to know: **identity theft** - a crime in which personal information (social security number, credit card, etc.) is stolen and used to gain credit, make purchases, obtain loans, etc.
                              scam - a scheme to swindle or cheat people

Procedure:

· While discussing the Springboard, explain that <u>what happened to David is called "identity theft"</u> (review term) <u>and can be perpetrated against ANYONE, even children, by ANYONE: strangers, friends, work associates, or even family members</u>. Go on to explain that <u>in this lesson the student(s) will learn more about identity theft and what can be done to avoid it.</u>

· Distribute the "Financial News Hour" handouts. **For group instruction** have the students read the skit in groups of three or have three students perform it. **For individual instruction** read the skit with your student or have him/her read it independently.

· Distribute "What to Know, What to Do" and have the student(s) complete the brainstorm organizer, doing further research as desired.

· Have them share answers and discuss. *(Answers may vary and include information about protecting from identity theft and what to do if it happens.)*

· Have the student(s) add examples to the "Assets and Liabilities" organizer. *(Assets include protecting social security numbers, shredding personal papers, monitoring credit cards for suspicious activity, etc. Liabilities include printing social security numbers on checks, putting bank statements or other paperwork in the trash, giving out ATM codes, computer passwords, or other personal information, etc.)*

· **EXTENSION**: Have student(s) create a public service announcement or pamphlet to inform others about how identity theft occurs and how to avoid it.

DAVID'S STORY

When David was five years old, his parents divorced, and he lived full time with his mother. A year later she remarried a man named Chuck Baylor. The next few years were neither happy nor stable for David, because the family moved so often. Every time Chuck lost his job, they would fall behind on rent and eventually be forced to move again. Though they somehow always managed to find a new apartment, David was bounced from school to school, constantly having to leave friends and make new ones.

Finally, David's mother grew tired of the turmoil in their lives and divorced Chuck. She worked very hard to pay for night school and eventually became a nurse's aid and earned a decent living. With some help from public assistance, David's mother was even able to purchase a small home when David was fourteen and starting high school. Things definitely improved! He was able to attend the same school for all four years and graduated with honors, allowing David to win almost enough scholarship money for four years of college.

Then one day he received horrible news. He filled out paperwork for a student loan to help cover his college living expenses and was told his low credit score made it impossible for him to get a loan! When shown a copy of his credit report, David saw that there were several unpaid and maxed-out credit cards in his name, but he had never even applied for a credit card! There was an auto loan that was never paid and several collections for utility bills and back rent.

David didn't understand! He had worked summers and paid cash for his ten-year-old used car and had never lived at any of the addresses mentioned! He called his mother in a panic; how could this have happened?!

What do you think has happened to ruin David's credit?

How do you think this situation will hurt him in the future?

What do you think he can do about this?

Do you think this could happen to you? Why or why not?

Financial News Hour

Characters:
Ima Moneymaker, Financial News Hour Host
Special Agent Stark Fax, F.B.I.
Willy Wisewallet, Credit rating expert

Ima - Good evening, Ladies and Gentlemen, and welcome to this edition of *Financial News Hour*. We are thrilled to have two very important guests with us tonight, and out topic is something every man, woman, and yes, child should know about -- identity theft. So, without further ado, let me introduce our experts. Our first guest is Special Agent Stark Fax with the Federal Bureau of Investigation. Welcome Special Agent, thank you so much for being here.

Fax - Thank you Ima, it's a pleasure.

Ima - And our second guest is an expert in all things having to do with credit ratings. Please welcome to the show Mr. Willy Wisewallet.

Willy - Thank you for having me, Ima.

Ima - Certainly. Now, I'd like to begin with Special Agent Fax. Agent Fax, can you tell our audience a little bit about identity theft?

Fax - Of course. The first point I should make is that identity theft is a CRIME! It occurs when a thief steals someone's personal information.

Ima - (*startled*) Oh my! What kind of personal information?

Fax - Often, they'll steal and use a social security number. Think about it. Whether you're are applying for a credit card, a home loan, a car loan, or even financing a couch, what do they ask you for? Your social security number! So if scumbags can get hold of it, they have what they need to open credit cards in your name or take out many other kinds of loans.

Willy - Ima, do you mind if I interrupt here? I just want to point out that EVERYONE has a social security number, even babies! Parents are required to apply for them when their babies are born in order to get a break on their income tax each year. So it isn't just adults who are at risk.

Ima - Good point, I had never thought about that!

Fax - It's true; and it's also true that identity theft is America's fastest-growing crime. Thieves steal and use personal information of over 10 million Americans every year!

Ima - I had no idea it was that bad! How do they get hold of the information?

Fax - Well, I can tell you part of the story, since the FBI only deals with such thefts at the corporate, or big business level.

Willy - And I can tell you more about how it happens to regular folks.

Ima - And we definitely need to hear about that, but let's let Special Agent Fax start us off.

Willy - Good idea; theft happens at the corporate level more often anyway.

Fax - Indeed, it does, and personal information is most often stolen when criminals break into the computer files of large companies. When those companies sell products to customers, they gather names, addresses, credit card numbers, and other information that is stored in databases.

Ima - But aren't those files secure?

Fax - (*sighs*) You would think so, but computer hackers always seem to be ahead of technology. They figure it out and steal all kinds of information from thousands of people and then use it or sell it to other thieves.

Ima - That's awful! I had heard of this before but didn't realize how it works.

Fax - There are other ways it can happen, too. Sometimes, the thieves actually work at a company, insiders if you will. These dirt bags gather information by taking it from computer records or in some cases steal it directly from files or even the trash.

Ima - So, how do you catch them?

Fax - Unless we have a witness or can track the files, it's very hard.

Willy - Unfortunately when identity theft occurs at the personal level, it's also very hard to catch the thief. After all, crooks don't use their own names!

Ima - Please tell use more about personal identity theft, Willy.

Willy - When it happens to an individual, it can be due to something as simple as having a thief peek over your shoulder at an ATM machine to see your personal identification number, or your pin. They can then pick your pocket, take your card to another ATM, and voila! They withdraw YOUR money!

Ima - Is that the most common way personal identity theft happens?

Willy - Oh no, I was just making a point of how easily people can be taken. Actually one of the most common ways identities are stolen is from trash cans.

Ima - (*surprised*) Really?!

Willy - Really. Thieves go through dumpsters and trash heaps to steal bank statements, credit card receipts, utility bills, you name it. If they can find personal information, they can use it to steal from the people who threw it away!

Fax - Just think of how much personal information is on people's monthly bills! And all it takes to avoid it falling into the wrong hands is a shredder! Truly, spending as little as $25 could save people thousands in the long run!

Willy - He's right, Ima. People should never just throw bills or other paperwork away without shredding it first.

Ima - Good advice! What else can you tell use about how identities get stolen?

Willy - There are many other ways it happens. Unfortunately, the Internet has helped make the crime much more common.

Fax - That's for sure! People don't realize how careful they need to be. They foolishly believe everything they read because it's on the (*makes air quotes*) "net."

Ima - Can you give us an example?

Fax - A common way it happens is called "phishing."

Ima - I'm guessing this has nothing to do with a pole and a hook?

Fax - No, phishing is when scammers set up what looks like a legitimate website for a bank or other business. Then they send out e-mails that lure people to go to that site and enter personal data.

Ima - Who would do that? And why?

Fax - Many people do it all the time because it looks real. Let's say you receive an email that looks like it's from your bank, saying they need to update your records. You follow the link, and the website it takes you to looks official, bank logo and everything. Sadly, many people fall for this scam, which gives a thief access to your account, which can then be emptied out!

Ima - That's very scary!

Willy - Excuse me, Ima, but I need to interrupt here.

Ima - Please, go right ahead.

Willy - The things we have discussed here are common tactics identity thieves use. Yet I also think we should make your audience aware that not all identity thieves are strangers.

Ima - Really?

Willy - Oh yes. In recent years we have seen quite an increase in children having their identities stolen.

Ima - That's terrible! You mentioned something earlier about social security numbers of babies being stolen. Is that what you are referring to?

Willy - I'm afraid so. We have even seen a number of cases of late. Parents or other relatives use children's information to open new accounts when they have bad credit or have reached their credit limits and need additional loans or credit cards.

Ima - That's awful! They ruin their own child's credit before the kid is even old enough to apply for a credit card or get a car loan!

Willy - Right, and because children don't need credit until their late teens or beyond, the abuse can go on for years before it's discovered.

Fax - I should add that this also happens with deceased relatives. Thieves scan newspaper death notices for the recently departed, do a little research, and BAM! They have a new identity to use for purchases, credit, and anything else.

Ima - That is unbelievable! Well, I think now that we've made our audience aware of how identity theft happens, we owe it to them to also offer advice on how to avoid it. Special Agent Fax, what advice do you have for our viewers?

Fax - One of the most important things you can do is to protect your social security number. Do not EVER have it printed on checks or write it down anywhere that is not secure. NEVER carry your social security card in your wallet in case it you should lose it or it is stolen; and NEVER give it to anyone on the phone or otherwise unless you know it's secure. Also, be careful when you're on your computer. Protect it with a password that isn't obvious and don't share it.

Ima - And Willy? What advice would you give?

Willy - Protect your trashcan and your mailbox. These are two places where thieves can get all kinds of paperwork with personal information. If you go on vacation, have the post office hold your mail or have a friend bring it in. Use drop boxes to mail your bills and like Agent Fax advised, USE YOUR SHREDDER!

Ima - Good advice, Gentlemen. Is there anything else you'd like to share before we end our program?

Fax - One last thing: I would advise people to photocopy everything they carry in their wallets; credit cards, drivers license, anything you have that if it were to be stolen, you would have all the information needed to cancel anything that could be used against you.

Willy - Absolutely! If you do lose your wallet, you should call your credit card companies and bank right away to let them know. They can cancel your account numbers so no one can use the cards or access your bank account.

Ima - Well, everything you've told us has been interesting and excellent advice! I want to thank our guests for their time and all their valuable information to make our audience aware of a horrible crime and what they can do to keep it from happening to them. That's another edition of Financial News Hour. Good night!

What To KNOW / What To DO

DIRECTIONS: Complete the organizer with information from the skit and your own ideas.

What should you **KNOW** about identity theft and how it happens?	What can you **DO** to avoid identity theft; and what should you **DO** if it happens to you?

Building a Nest Egg

Springboard:
Students should respond to the "When I'm Old and Grey" questions.
(Answers will vary but should be reflective and spark discussion.)

Objective: The student will be able to describe various types of savings and investment options.

Materials: When I'm Old and Grey (Springboard handout)
                        Savings and Investments (handout)

Terms to know: **retirement** - when someone permanently stops working for a living
                        investment - money spent in hopes of future gains
                        return - the amount of profit made
                        maturation - endpoint of an investment period

Procedure:

- After discussing the Springboard questions, explain that *investing and saving money wisely throughout your lifetime will increase your chances of having a comfortable and enjoyable retirement*. Go on to explain that *in this lesson the student(s) will conduct research to learn more about various types of investments*.
- **For group instruction** have the students divide into teams of no more than five students. Distribute "Savings and Investments" and have the teams conduct Internet research about each term. Then the teams should write at least ten questions about the material.
- When the teams are finished, *announce that they will now participate in a team challenge*. Review the following rules for the challenge:
  - Teams take turns challenging another team with a question.
  - The challenged team has 10 seconds to answer correctly for 10 points. If they can't answer correctly, the challenging team gets 15 points.
  - No team may be challenged twice in a row.
  - A team not challenged in 5 turns automatically answers the next question.
  - The team with the most points at the end of the game wins.
- **For individualized instruction** the student and parent/teacher should challenge each other for points.
- Have the student(s) play the quiz game for as long as desired and then add examples to their "Assets and Liabilities" organizer. *(Assets would be investing wisely, saving for retirement, understanding investments, etc. Liabilities include not investing or saving money, risky investments, "get rich quick" schemes, etc.)*
- **EXTENSION:** The student(s) could interview a retired person for advice about the kinds of things they should be doing to prepare for a comfortable retirement; lessons they've learned; etc.

When I'm Old and Grey

DIRECTIONS: Think of someone you know who is retired or imagine your own retirement to respond to the following questions.

Describe what you think it is like to be retired. _____

_____

_____

_____

_____

_____

_____

What are some problems retired people might face?_____

_____

_____

_____

_____

_____

_____

What expenses do you think cost LESS for retirees? Why? _____

_____

_____

_____

_____

_____

_____

What expenses do you think cost MORE for retirees? Why? _____

_____

_____

_____

_____

_____

_____

Savings and Investments

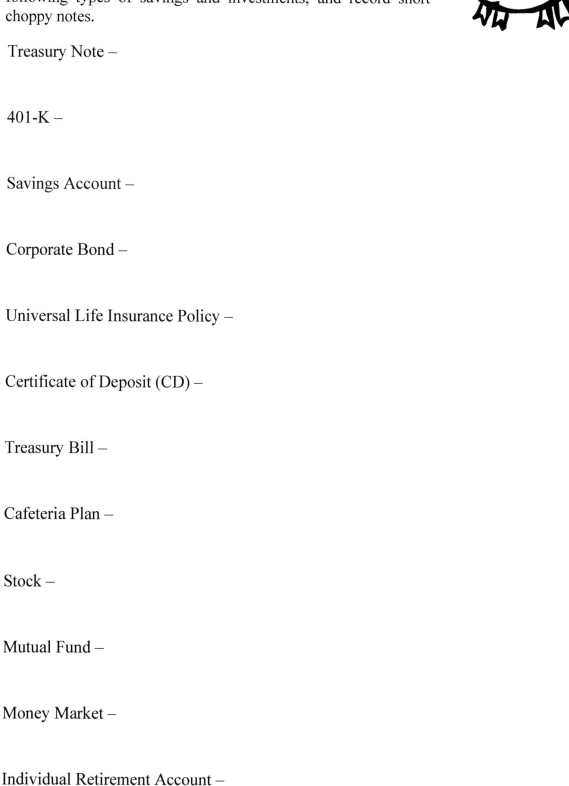

DIRECTIONS: Use the Internet to briefly research the following types of savings and investments, and record short choppy notes.

Treasury Note –

401-K –

Savings Account –

Corporate Bond –

Universal Life Insurance Policy –

Certificate of Deposit (CD) –

Treasury Bill –

Cafeteria Plan –

Stock –

Mutual Fund –

Money Market –

Individual Retirement Account –

Treasury Note – *This is a coupon issued by the federal government at a discount off the face value in denominations from $100 to $1,000,000. Maturation dates range from 2 to 10 years and interest is paid on a yearly basis. They are not worth their face value until they "mature," or reach the end of the term agreed upon.*

401-K – *Employees can have some of their paycheck set aside before income taxes are calculated into this type of account; some employers match part or all employee contributions. Money in the account is invested on behalf of the employee, and the funds can grow if the investments do well. If not, these accounts can lose value.*

Savings Account – *This is a personal bank account to which money can be easily deposited and withdrawn. The money earns small amounts of interest monthly based on how much is in the account, and usually no minimum balance required.*

Corporate Bond – *Similar to a Treasury note or bill, these are not backed by the federal government but are issued by a private company.*

Universal Life Insurance Policy – *Part of the premiums (monthly payments) for this life insurance policy are collected as cash value. Interest is then earned on the accumulated cash, which can be borrowed, cashed in, or added to the death benefit when the insured person dies.*

Certificate of Deposit (CD) – *CD's are issued by banks; the investor deposits a fixed sum of money for a defined period of time (as short as a few months or as long as many years). If the money is withdrawn before the date of maturity, fees are charged. CD's usually pay higher interest rates than savings accounts or money markets.*

Treasury Bill – *This coupon issued by the federal government is sold at a discount off the face value and matures in a year or less. No interest is paid until the maturity date.*

Cafeteria Plan – *This employer-based program allows people to set aside earnings before income taxes are calculated into an account that can be used to pay child care or medical bills.*

Stock – *Investors can buy these shares of ownership in a corporation, earning money when the stock is sold at a higher price per share than it was purchased. If the selling price is below the purchase price, money is lost.*

Mutual Fund – *Thousands of small investors' money is pooled together and invested in the stock market. The rate of return is relatively low because the risk of losing large amounts of money is low; but money can be lost as when investing in stock.*

Money Market – *Similar to a savings account, but these have a minimum (or higher minimum) balance. Limited withdrawals can be made over a period of time, and it pays higher interest than a savings account, depending upon the account balance.*

Individual Retirement Account – *Also known as a type of "annuity," money can be set aside for retirement (individually without an employer) in an account. The money is then invested, but the owner is guaranteed not to lose their original investment; returns generally lower since the account is less risky than a 401K.*

Choosing the Best

Springboard:
      Students should read "Risk vs. Return" and answer the questions.
(Answers will vary but should be justified and spark discussion.)

Objective: The student will be able to explain the relationship between risk and return in regards to investments.

Materials:
    Risk vs. Return (Springboard handout)
    Risky Business? (handout)
    Savings and Investments (from previous lesson)

Procedure:

- After reviewing the Springboard, explain that *in this lesson the student(s) will learn more about the risks involved in various types of investments*.

- Distribute the "Risky Business?" handout and have the student(s) work individually or in pairs to complete their continuum placements as instructed. They should use their "Savings and Investments" notes from the previous lesson for reference.

- Have them share their placements and discuss the relationship between how risky they perceived investments to be and the potential returns. (*Answers may vary somewhat, however generally the higher the risk, the higher the possible return. Savings accounts, money markets and treasury bills and notes are fairly low risk; IRA's and Mutual Funds are medium risk; stocks, corporate bonds, and 401K's are higher risks. All student placements should be justified.*)

- Hold a discussion, including the following questions:
  - **?** What are some investments you could make NOW, at this point in your life? *(savings accounts, CD's, treasury notes)*
  - **?** Why do you think investing would be a smart financial decision? *(Answers will vary but most people need more than their lifetime earnings to retire comfortably. If they invest, they should have more money to live.)*
  - **?** What do you think the phrase "making your money work for you" means? *(It means using your money to make more money through investment.)*

- Have the student(s) add examples to the "Assets and Liabilities" organizer. (*Assets would be making investments carefully while considering how much you can risk to lose, making your money work for you, building investments like a pyramid, etc.; liabilities include making too many risky investments, making risky investments too late in life, not taking any risk at all, etc.*)

Risk v$. Return

When considering how to invest your money, "risk" refers to the chance of making or losing money on your investment. Some forms of investment pose very little risk because you cannot lose the money you originally invested. On the other hand some investments are very risky because not only could you not make money, but you could lose everything.

How much to invest and how to invest it depends on many factors. For example people who have little cash or other assets should probably not choose high risk investments because they could lose the little money they have. However, people who have a lot of cash or extra money that is not needed to meet basic needs can afford to take greater chances with their investments. Another factor to consider is how close a person is to retirement when making investment decisions. A high risk investment might result in someone losing everything when they are about to leave the work force and have little means to earn more money. In general most investment counselors and other experts advise people to think of their investments as a pyramid: the largest portion, or the base, should be in safe investments with a much smaller amount of money at the high-risk level.

The other factor to consider when investing is the potential return on the money. Basically, lower risk investments earn less money. The reward then for risky investments is the chance to make larger sums, but there is no guarantee. However, experts also advise against not taking risk at all, because no risk means little to no return on your money.

Describe a person who you think should NOT choose a high risk investment. _____
_____
_____
_____

Describe a person who you think SHOULD choose a high risk investment.
_____
_____
_____

What other factors do you think should be considered when making investments? _____
_____
_____
_____

Risky Business?

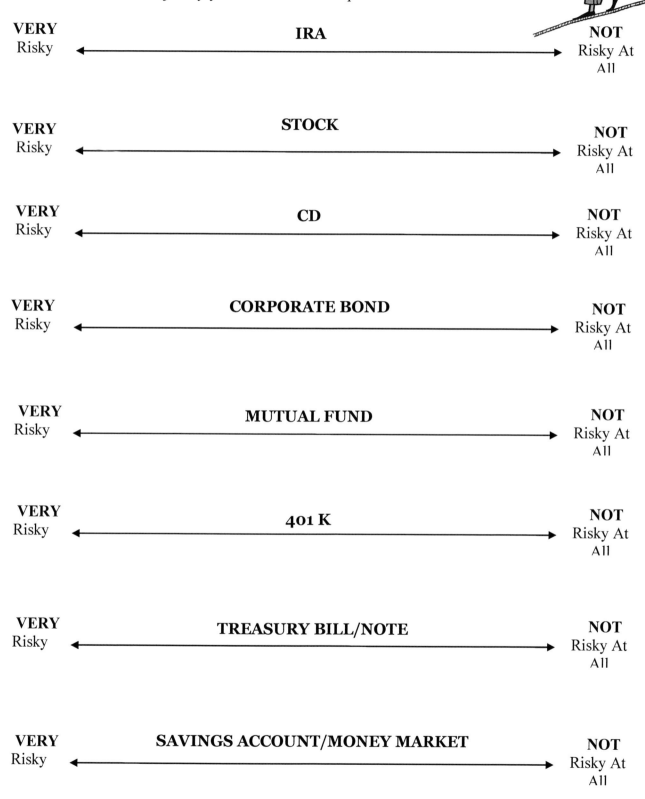

DIRECTIONS: Mark an X on the line to show where you think each type of investment falls. Then justify your answers in the space below.

IRA

VERY
Risky ← → NOT
Risky At
All

STOCK

VERY
Risky ← → NOT
Risky At
All

CD

VERY
Risky ← → NOT
Risky At
All

CORPORATE BOND

VERY
Risky ← → NOT
Risky At
All

MUTUAL FUND

VERY
Risky ← → NOT
Risky At
All

401 K

VERY
Risky ← → NOT
Risky At
All

TREASURY BILL/NOTE

VERY
Risky ← → NOT
Risky At
All

SAVINGS ACCOUNT/MONEY MARKET

VERY
Risky ← → NOT
Risky At
All

CRASH!

Springboard:
Students should study "The Business Cycle" and answer the questions.
(*Answers will vary but could include: recession conditions include lack of money, loss of jobs, lost investments, poverty, etc; recovery conditions include more buying and selling, new jobs, wealth made, investments doing well, etc.*)

Objective: The student will be able to explain how the business cycle can affect people's lives.

Materials: The Business Cycle (Springboard handout)
Ups and Downs (2 pages of cards - cut out and shuffled)
poster board or butcher paper (optional)

Terms to know: **economy** - the financial activity of a nation, state, community, the world, etc.
recession - time period of poor economic conditions
foreclosure - loss of a home due to failure to make mortgage payments

Procedure:

· After reviewing the Springboard, explain that _this lesson looks at how changes in the business cycle affect our lives._

· **For group instruction** students can work in pairs or small groups with one set of cut out and shuffled "Ups and Downs" cards to per pair or group. Students should collaborate to figure out where on the business cycle they think each event or condition would occur and put them in the most logical order possible. **For individualized instruction** the student should sort and order the cards independently or with parent/teacher help.

· If desired, have the student(s) draw and label the business cycle on a large piece of poster board or butcher paper and glue the cards along the curve where they think they should go.

· Have the student(s) share / compare their ideas and discuss. (*Answers may vary somewhat, but in general the items on the first page of cards occur during a recession and those on the second page occur during recovery and peak times.*)

· Have the student(s) add lesson examples to the "Assets and Liabilities" organizer. (*Assets include preparing for economic downtimes by saving money, not mounting a lot of debt, etc. Liabilities would be losing work during a recession, not preparing for downtimes by saving, etc.*)

· **EXTENSION:** Have the student(s) briefly research the most recent recession and report on how that crisis affected people.

THE BUSINESS CYCLE

The business cycle refers to the ups and downs in the economy. It is not regular or predictable but in general it flows as shown.

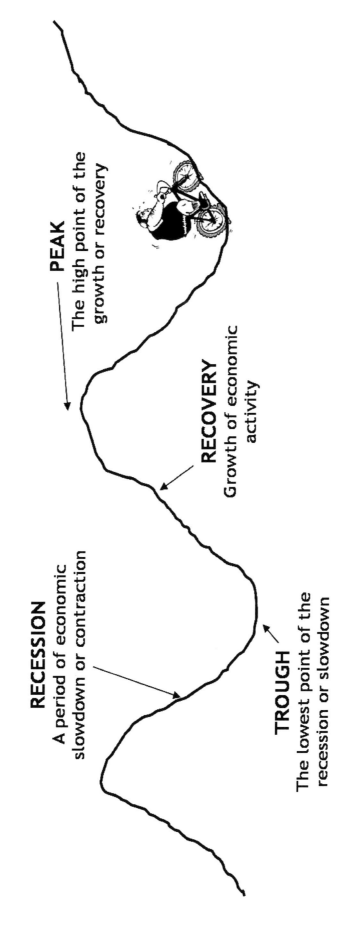

PEAK
The high point of the growth or recovery

RECOVERY
Growth of economic activity

RECESSION
A period of economic slowdown or contraction

TROUGH
The lowest point of the recession or slowdown

What do you think conditions are like during recessions?

What do you think conditions are like during recovery periods?

Ups and Downs

People can no longer afford to pay their mortgages.	Homes are foreclosed on in large numbers.
People use up the money in their savings accounts and other assets to live.	People live paycheck to paycheck, never having enough to save anything.
People lose their jobs in large numbers.	There are so many people looking for work, it is very hard to find a job.
People feel uncertain and fearful about their futures.	The stock market values go down as people sell their shares out of fear.
The value of investments goes down, causing many people to lose money.	The number of bankruptcies rises.
People stop spending money on vacations, eating out, home improvement, etc.	Many people's credit ratings go down.
People avoid making large purchases, such as cars.	Banks slow their lending to people by making it MUCH harder to qualify for loans.
More people have to go on public assistance (welfare, food stamps, etc.)	People stop investing and hold onto whatever money they have.
People stop shopping and buying; many companies go out of business.	People lose their health insurance and other benefits.
More people lose their homes and become homeless.	Alcoholism, drug abuse, and divorce rates all rise.

⬆ Ups and Downs ⬇

New business begin to open and thrive.	More jobs become available; people can find work easily.
Wages go up and people have more money to spend or save.	It becomes easier to get loans from banks or other lenders.
Home prices rise and people make more from home sales.	The stock market booms as many people are buying and selling.
Retail sales rise as people shop till they drop!	People begin to use credit more freely.
Business owners get rich as their companies' profits rise.	People earn big returns from their investments.
People begin to spend and invest money more freely.	People feel confident and have greater hope for the future.
More homes are bought and sold.	People buy big-ticket items such as cars, boats, etc.
People tend to overextend themselves, spending more than they make.	Savings accounts grow as more people have extra money each month.
People spend money on luxuries such as vacations, eating at nice restaurants, etc.	People's credit ratings go up.
People make riskier investments since they have more money to risk.	Overall, the economy grows as people are working, buying, selling, and investing.

Springboard:
Students should highlight the three most important assets and three most important liabilities on their organizers and explain their choices on the back.
(*Answers will vary but should be justified.*)

Objective: The student will write a reflective essay about good and bad financial habits that they have studied in this unit.

Materials: Assets and Liabilities (completed unit organizer)
Reflective Writing (handout)
Setting Your Goals (from previous lesson; page 10)
Reflective Web (handout)
Reflection on Reflection (rubric)

Terms to know: **reflection** - thinking back on what has been learned or accomplished to gain knowledge for the future

Procedure:

· After reviewing the Springboard, explain that *in this lesson the student(s) will reflect back upon goals they identified at the beginning of the unit and what they have learned that could help meet those goals*.

· Distribute copies of "Reflective Writing." Read over the information. (**F.Y.I.** Reflective writing is usually done either as a diary entry or an essay. The essay format is presented here, but you could simplify the lesson by having them write a diary page instead.)

· The student(s) should use "Setting Your Goals" and their organizers to refer to while writing their essays. (A web form is provided for organizational help.)

· The student(s) should then plan and write the papers, remembering to include an introductory paragraph outlining what is to be discussed and a summary paragraph, reemphasizing the main points. Allow as much time as you feel is appropriate. You can assign it purely for reflective purposes or as a formal writing assignment. (The "Reflection on Reflection" rubric is provided for assessment.)

· The student(s) should be given an opportunity to share insights they gain from their reflection.

REFLECTIVE WRITING

What Is It?

Reflective writing is "a written personal analysis of past learning experiences and feelings that provides an opportunity for knowledge and a guide for future actions." While that definition seems complex, it really isn't. What it means is that in reflective writing a student examines the past in order to learn from it. Reflecting on what has been learned and experienced allows a person to learn from both successes and failures. Successful actions and learning can be repeated, and similar mistakes can be avoided.

Certainly thinking about the past is useful, but writing about it can be even more so. Organizing thoughts to put on paper requires a high level of analysis. In considering what to write, a student must think carefully about what he or she did and has learned: Why have they set the goals that they have? What do they want their future to look like, and how can good financial habits help them get there? What actions have they taken that demonstrate good or poor financial habits? How important are these habits in helping reach their goals? These are the kinds of questions that are answered in reflective writing.

How Is It Done?

Reflective writing should go well beyond a simple description of information or events. It should also describe the writer's feelings about experiences and reactions to what was learned. Because reflective writing is a "personal analysis," it is often written in "first person." Unlike many other written forms, the use of words such as "I," "we," or "my" is preferred.

For this assignment, the writer should think about how he/she answered personal questions throughout the unit. For example when studying spending habits, how did the student score on the survey? How have the student's opinions changed regarding the use of credit or the importance of budgeting?

What Should Be Included?

Here is a list of questions that could be answered in the reflective writing:

? What are the goals that were set at the beginning of the unit?

? What are the most important things that will help you meet those goals?

? Why is it helpful to set goals this early in life?

? What opinions have changed about certain topics after completing the lessons, and how have they changed?

? What habits will likely be changed or developed in the future, and why?

? Which lessons were most informative and helpful, and why?

? How will this new knowledge change future behaviors?

… etc.

Reflective Web

Select three or four questions to explore in your reflective essay. Record your thoughts about each on the web below, and use those notes to write a paragraph about each point. Remember to begin the essay with an introductory paragraph and end with a summary.

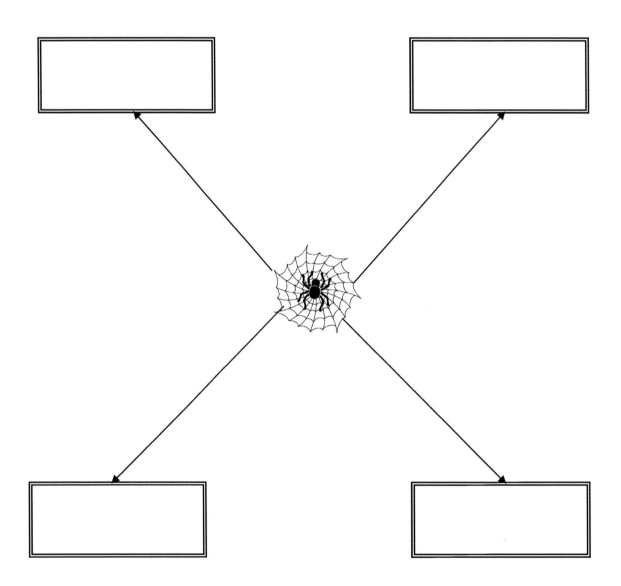

Reflection on Reflection

Name _____

Use the following scale to evaluate your reflective essay:

4 - excellent   2 - fair   0 - unacceptable
3 - good   1 - poor

	student	teacher
Provides a clear introduction	_____	_____
Includes thoughtful personal analysis	_____	_____
Includes discussion of goals	_____	_____
Includes relevant financial habits	_____	_____
Provides clear details explaining each point	_____	_____
Summarizes information in final paragraph	_____	_____
Spelling and grammar	_____	_____

GRADE

COMMENTS:

Reflection on Reflection

Name _____

Use the following scale to evaluate your reflective essay:

4 - excellent   2 - fair   0 - unacceptable
3 - good   1 - poor

	student	teacher
Provides a clear introduction	_____	_____
Includes thoughtful personal analysis	_____	_____
Includes discussion of goals	_____	_____
Includes relevant financial habits	_____	_____
Provides clear details explaining each point	_____	_____
Summarizes information in final paragraph	_____	_____
Spelling and grammar	_____	_____

GRADE

COMMENTS:

$$ Reviewing Term$ $$

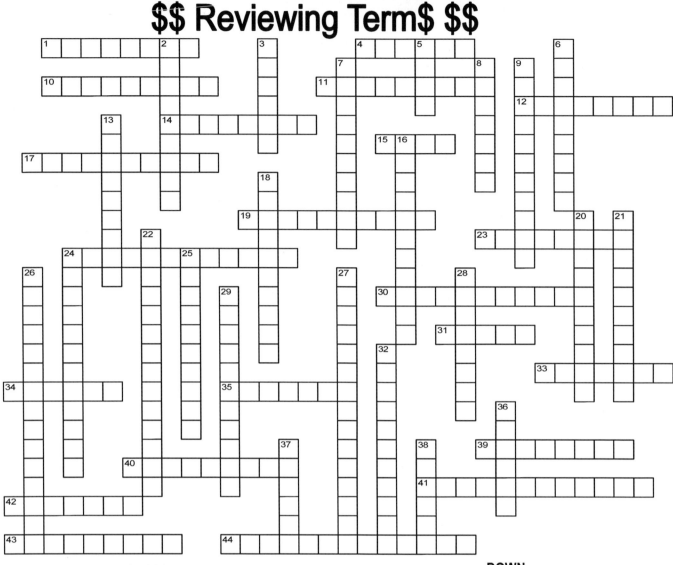

ACROSS

1 salary list based on education, experience, etc.
4 plan for spending
10 money taken out of an account
11 protection against theft, harm, illness, death, etc.
12 store or business that sells to the public
14 charge for borrowed money
15 scheme to swindle people
17 money paid for percentages of sales
19 position for learning a profession
23 money borrowed to buy a house
24 statement of a person's credit score
30 one who makes decisions about loan applications
31 factor that contributes to meeting a goal
33 financial activity of a nation, etc.
34 pay at regular intervals over a year
35 fees for schooling
39 employer-paid insurance, day care, etc.
40 misleading
41 fees and other costs at the time money is borrowed
42 recommend
43 period of a poor economy
44 crime of using personal information to steal

DOWN

2 factor that stands in one's way of achieving goals
3 occupation
5 to be achieved
6 itemized list of account information
7 money spent in hopes of future earnings
8 money put into an account
9 loss of a home due to failure to pay the mortgage
13 gas, electricity, and water
16 3-digit summary of one's finances and payment history
18 court proceeding to settle with creditors for one who cannot pay debts
20 end of an investment period
21 means of learning from the past
22 bills and day-to-day costs
24 evaluation of a person's spending history and habits
25 time when a person no longer works for a living
26 money decisions a person makes that affect security
27 day-to-day bank account
28 one who buys goods or services
29 percentage of the poor
32 money paid toward a credit purchase
36 buy now; pay later
37 profit on an investment
38 money earned from work

$$ Reviewing Term$ $$
Puzzle Answer$

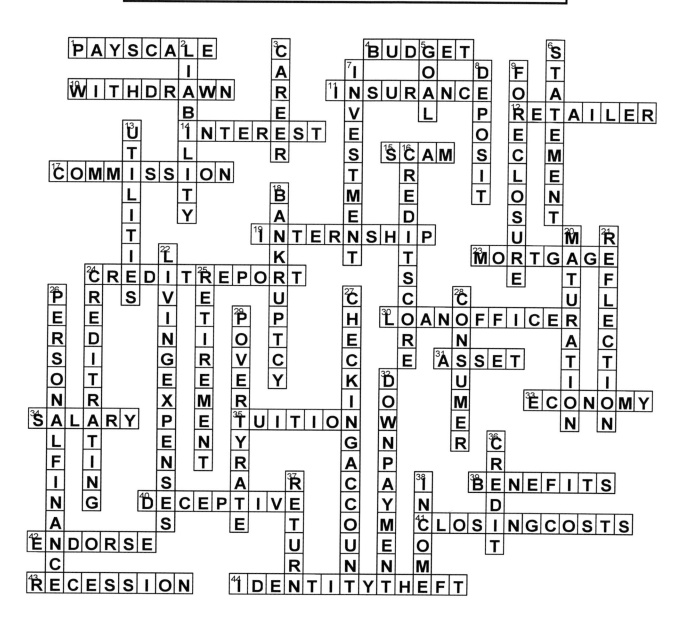

Personal Finance (A)

Fill in the blanks with unit terms from the word bank:

budget	loan officer	maturation	interest
salary	insurance	consumer	retirement
mortgage	deposit	credit score	endorsement

1. A person who buys goods and services is a/an _____.
2. Keeping a/an _____ helps track expenses and spending.
3. The actress gave a strong _____ for the shampoo.
4. It is important to buy_____ to protect a home or car.
5. The couple was approved for the _____ to buy a house.
6. The man made a $500 _____ into his checking account.
7. Borrowers must pay _____ on any loans they take out.
8. At _____, money can be taken from the fund with interest.
9. The old man has gone fishing every day since his _____.
10. The young woman's low _____ kept her from buying a new car.

Give an example of each:

11. goal - _____
12. investment - _____
13. income - _____
14. retailer - _____
15. career - _____

Multiple Choice - Write the letter of the correct answer in the blank:

16. ____ Which of these is **NOT** a type of expense?
    A. fixed   C. informational
    B. variable   D. discretionary
17. ____ When paying bills, most people use their
    A. checking account.   C. money market.
    B. down payments   .   D. mutual funds.
18. ____ All of these actions can help protect your identity, **EXCEPT**
    A. shredding bank statements and other paperwork.
    B. using a private password to protect your computer.
    C. stopping your mail when you go on a vacation or trip.
    D. carrying your social security card with you at all times.
19. ____ The economy slows and affects people in negative ways during a
    A. peak.   B. recession.   C. boom.   D. recovery.

Fully answer the following question:

20. Explain two ways that using credit cards can be harmful.

*"To you, it may be the holiday season. To me, it's the danger season. I'm talking about the five weeks between Thanksgiving and Christmas, when 20 percent of our country's annual retail spending occurs. Jamming one-fifth of our spending into a frenzied window of shopping time can lead to some ugly financial results: A whole lot of bills we have no way of paying off come January ... The absolute worst move you can make is to charge gifts on a credit card you can't afford to pay off. If you run up a $1,000 balance this holiday season ... and you intend to pay it off slowly each month by making minimum payments, your interest charges will total around $1,000 if your card has an 18 percent rate. In other words, your total gift spending will double. That's just financially irresponsible ... When you're standing at a checkout counter and the clerk offers you a 10 percent discount if you agree to open a store credit card account, say no. It's a **multifaceted** trap. First, it seems to be human nature that you'll use that 10 percent discount as an excuse to buy more... you'll end up spending more than you intended when you first stepped up to the cash register....And by the way, if you open up a bunch of retail cards for the supposed 10 percent discount "deal," you can end up hurting your (credit) score; remember, part of your score is dependent on whether you've obtained new credit over the past 12 months."*

(Excerpt from "Five Ways to Avoid Holiday Overspending," Suze Orman, *Money Matters*, 11-17-06)

21. ____ The word "multifaceted" **MOST NEARLY** means
   A. unlikely.
   B. many-sided.
   C. often misused.
   D. semi-annual.

22. ____ Which of these comments would the reading's author **MOST** agree with?
   A. People shouldn't buy gifts for their friends and family for holidays.
   B. Consumers are less likely to use credit wisely when buying gifts.
   C. Shoppers should try to limit the number of credit cards they have.
   D. It helpful for store owners to ruin their shopper's credit ratings.

23. ____ The **BEST** title for this passage would be
   A. "Holidays can be Hazardous for Shoppers."
   B. "Stores Offer Shoppers Holiday Bargains."
   C. "Say No to Credit Cards for the Holidays."
   D. "Shop Early and Avoid the Holiday Rush."

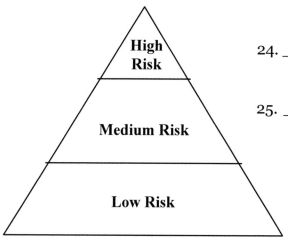

24. ____ The graphic on the left shows a plan for
   A. investment.
   B. college.
   C. retirement.
   D. budgeting.

25. ____ According to the graphic, most action should be at the ___ risk level, with the least action at the ___ risk level.
   A. high ... medium
   B. medium ... low
   C. low ... medium
   D. low ... high

Personal Finance (B)

Fill in the blanks with unit terms:
1. The doctor treated thousands of patients over her long _____.
2. The couple saved money to make a _____ on a new home.
3. The man's _____ showed many late payments on his bills.
4. The salesperson earned a big _____ for selling that car!
5. The football player's _____ of sport shoes caused sales to soar.
6. Staying on a/an_____ can help prevent overspending.
7. The couple was approved for the _____ to buy a house.
8. Shoppers must be careful to avoid being victims of _____.
9. According to the _____, more education earns more money.
10. The old man has gone fishing every day since his _____.

Give an example of each:
11. investment - _____
12. benefit - _____
13. asset - _____
14. deceptive advertising - _____
15. liability - _____

Multiple Choice - write the letter of the correct answer in the blank:
16. ____ Which of these situations would **NOT** help thieves steal an identity?
    A. An old man enters his personal information on an unverified website.
    B. Mail piles up in your neighbor's mailbox for three days straight.
    C. A student tells some buddies his ATM code to help him remember it.
    D. The clerk copied everything in her wallet to store in a safe place.

17. ____ These are all the family's ____ expenses, **EXCEPT** the ____.
    A. fixed ... grocery bill   C. monthly ... house payment
    B. variable ... car payment   D. income ... car insurance

18. ____ Which event is **NOT** likely to happen during a recession?
    A. many people lose their jobs
    B. the stock market booms
    C. homes go into foreclosure
    D. retail sales are very low

19. ____ In most cases high rates of return come with
    A. older retirement.   C. greater risks.
    B. longer maturations.   D. savings accounts.

Fully answer the following question on your own paper and attach:
20. Explain two personal finance decisions that would be assets and two liabilities for having a comfortable life.

Personal Finance (C)

Complete the analogies with unit terms:

1. Month is to job, as thirty years is to _____.
2. Auto loan is to car, as _____ is to a house.
3. Internship is to the beginning, as _____ is to the end.
4. Peak is to trough, as extreme wealth is to _____.
5. Import is to export, as_____ is to expenses.
6. Rise is to deposit, as diminish is to _____.
7. Eviction is to renting, as _____ is to a home ownership.
8. Premium is to insurance, as _____ is to college.
9. Recovery is to up-tick, as _____ is to downturn.
10. Wages are to hourly, as _____ is to yearly.

Give an example of each:

11. internship - _____
12. commission - _____
13. deceptive advertisement - _____
14. scam - _____
15. endorsement - _____

Multiple Choice - write the letter of the correct answer in the blank:

16. ____ Showing care with ____ is an asset to preventing ____.
    A. personal finances ... investments
    B. financial information ... identity theft
    C. checking accounts ... low living expenses
    D. account maturation ... a high poverty rate

17. ____ These are all the family's ____ expenses, **EXCEPT** the ____.
    A. variable ... grocery bill   C. monthly ... doctor bills
    B. fixed ... car payment   D. income ... car insurance

18. ____ During a recession, it is **UNLIKELY** that
    A. banks would foreclose on many loans.
    B. families would go on fewer vacations.
    C. many people would lose their jobs.
    D. the stock market would skyrocket.

19. ____ A man starting a new job at age fifty-nine should choose to invest
    A. a lot of money in high risk stocks to get rich quick.
    B. in funds that offer lower returns but have lower risk.
    C. his savings is new companies with hopes for success.
    D. in a high risk, high yield 401K to maximize his profits.

Fully answer the following question on your own paper and attach:

20. Explain two personal finance decisions that would be assets and two liabilities for having a comfortable life.

Form A:
1. consumer
2. budget
3. endorsement
4. insurance
5. mortgage
6. deposit
7. interest
8. maturation
9. retirement
10. credit score

11. college, good job, own a house, etc.
12. stock market, treasury notes, mutual funds, etc.
13. salary, wages, benefits, commissions, etc.
14. Gap, WalMart, gas station, pet shop, etc.
15. doctor, lawyer, accountant, teacher, etc.
16. C
17. A
18. D
19. B
20. Answers will vary; can get overspend, buy thing you cannot afford, have to pay high interest, could result in bad credit, etc.

Form B:
1. career
2. down payment
3. credit score/report
4. commission
5. endorsement
6. budget
7. mortgage
8. scams, identity theft
9. pay scale
10. retirement

11. stock market, treasury notes, mutual funds, etc.
12. company car, health insurance, day care, etc.
13. saving for the future, education, not overspending, etc.
14. bait and switch, false pricing, false sales, etc.
15. late payments, bankruptcy, unstable employment, etc.
16. D
17. A
18. B
19. C
20. Answers will vary; assets could be good credit, savings, investments, education; liabilities could be overspending, identity theft, debt, etc.

Form C:
1. career
2. mortgage
3. retirement
4. bankruptcy
5. income
6. withdrawal
7. foreclosure
8. tuition
9. recession
10. salary

11. advertising, communications, politics, etc.
12. for selling a house, car, insurance policy, etc.
13. bait and switch, false pricing, false sales, etc.
14. phishing, bait and switch, swampland in Florida, etc.
15. football player, actress, etc. LOVES a product
16. B
17. C
18. D
19. B
20. Answers will vary; assets could be good credit, savings, investments, education; liabilities could be overspending, identity theft, debt, etc.

Skills Forms A-C:
21. B
22. C
23. A
24. A
25. D

RESOURCES

www.investopedia.com/?viewed=1 - Investopedia Your Source for Investing Education, 2009.

money.cnn.com/pf/ - Personal finance advice and news, CNNmoney.com, 2009.

www.moneyinstructor.com/ - Money Instructor, Money Personal Finance, Business Careers, Life Skills: Lessons, education, 2009.

financialplan.about.com/od/personalfinancebasics/Personal Finance and Money Management Basics.htm - Personal Finance and Money Management Basics, about.com, 2009.

www.efunda.com/formulae/finance/loan calculator.cfm - loan calculators, efunda.com, 2009.

money.howstuffworks.com/personal-finance/debt-management/credit-score.htm - "How Credit Scores Work," howstuffworks.com, 2009.

www.councilforeconed.org/ - The Council for Economic Education, 2009.

www.jumpstartcoalition,org - The Jumpstart Coalition for Personal Financial Literacy, 2009.

www.kidsbank.com - Sovereign Bank Presents Kidsbank.com, 2009.

ecedweb.unomaha.edu/K-12/home.cfm - Econweb - Economic Education Web, 2009.

www.federalreserve.gov/ - The Federal Reserve System of the United States homepage, 2009.

www.econdata.net/ - econdata.net, 2009.

www.nationalsms.com/ -National Stock Market simulations, Stock Track Group Inc, 2009.

classroomedition.com/cre/ - The Wall Street Journal Classroom Edition, 2009.

www.fte.org/ - Foundation for Teaching Economics, 2008

I Think - Thematic Units

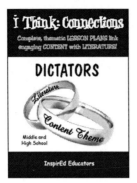

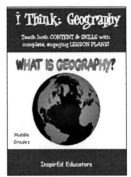

Some of our other **I Think** offerings include:

Series	Titles
I Think: Connections	Civilization, Democracy, Dictators, Ethnic Conflict, Indigenous People, Imperialism
I Think: U.S. History	Colonial America, American Revolution, Westward Expansion, The Civil War, Reconstruction Era, Problems & Progressives, The Modern Era
I Think: Government	Electing the President, Civic Participation. The Constitution, The Executive, Legislative, and Judicial Branches
I Think: Geography	What Is Geography?, U.S. Regions, World Geography by Region
I Think: World History	Ancient Civilizations, Middle Ages, Renaissance, the World Wars, etc.
I Think: Economics	What Is Economics? Personal Finance
I Think: Reading & Writing	Poetry, Short Stories, Literary Themes, Novels, Biographies, etc.
I Think: I Can!	Early Learning Thematics

We're adding more titles all the time.
Check our websites for current listings!

www.inspirededucators.com

www.inspiredhomeschoolers.com